1978

The Donald Rogers
Illustrated Handbook of
Arts and Crafts Lesson Plans
for the Elementary Teacher:

AN INNOVATIVE CLASSROOM-TESTED APPROACH

The Donald Rogers Illustrated Handbook of Arts and Crafts Lesson Plans for the Elementary Teacher:

AN INNOVATIVE CLASSROOM-TESTED APPROACH

DONALD ROGERS

PARKER PUBLISHING COMPANY, Inc.

WEST NYACK, NEW YORK

Library of Congress Cataloging in Publication Data

Rogers, Donald,
    The Donald Rogers illustrated handbook of arts and
crafts lesson plans for the elementary teacher.

    Includes index.
    1. Handicraft—Study and teaching (Elementary)
I. Title.
TT150.R63   372.5'044   76-24823
ISBN 0-13-218396-X

Printed in the United States of America

INTRODUCTION

This illustrated handbook of arts and crafts lesson plans is a practical book of ideas tested in the classroom by elementary teachers who were not art specialists. During the classroom testing phase of the manuscript, many activities were modified and adjusted to meet the needs of a self-contained elementary classroom, where the lessons would be taught. Skills, techniques and objectives of the lessons were refitted to the basic art materials available in most elementary schools.

Readers will find the stages of each art activity fully illustrated and readily understandable. Teachers will be able to identify the concepts of a lesson, at a glance, from these pictorial steps. Used in conjunction with the "How-To-Do-It" sections of each activity, the illustrations provide all the necessary information about preparation of the class, motivation, tools and materials, sequence of the activity and cleaning up after the lesson.

Each chapter in the book is devoted to a different basic art material, following a development from simple concepts and activities to more complicated and comprehensive activities. Common problems that are encountered when using each art material are discussed carefully and solutions are offered. Lists of materials and tools required to teach each activity are found at the beginning of each lesson. Practical suggestions about substitute materials help to make the lessons more flexible for classroom teachers who have limited access to supplies. Indeed, materials "found" around the house are an important part of both the arts and crafts sections of the book.

Carefully prepared charts, listing the concepts, emotional and intellectual experiences, physical skills and new skills introduced, are at the beginning of each chapter of the book. Classroom teachers will find both the charts and illustrations useful in creating their own modifications of the activities. These changes are vital since each classroom is different and the experiences, interests and background of elementary school pupils vary greatly, particularly in the area of selecting subjects or themes for an activity.

Demonstrations in the use of art materials have been minimized for those classroom teachers who do not feel secure in using a variety of media. Art activities in this book rely upon motivating pupils through group discussion and questions. Key questions that other classroom teachers have found successful are included in the text of each activity. Teachers will find it easy to adapt these verbal motivations to their own classroom.

This handbook is a practical resource for everyday use. Over a hundred time-tested art activities, ranging from teaching simple spatial concepts to creating large sculptural forms are introduced simply for the classroom teacher. This book is a complete guide for both the beginning teacher and the experienced one. The range, from learning the principles of drawing to building large wooden sculpture is more than the usual elementary art book offers.

Donald Rogers

CONTENTS

4. Printing Different Things *(Continued)*

5. Creating With Paper 118

6. Working With Wood 148

8. Found Material Ideas (*Continued*)

The Donald Rogers
Illustrated Handbook of
Arts and Crafts Lesson Plans
for the Elementary Teacher:
AN INNOVATIVE CLASSROOM-TESTED APPROACH

CHAPTER 1

Learning to Draw Things

INTRODUCTION TO DRAWING

All children learn to scribble and draw simple symbols before they begin formal schooling. Some pupils enjoy drawing more than others but, like singing, drawing is fun until it becomes work. Unfortunately, children draw more out-of-school than they do in school. This frequently occurs because the subjects motivated are of more interest to the teacher than to children themselves. Strike when the interest is hot!

Topics or themes used for drawing should be a product of a child's own thinking. This thinking requires some stimulation from the teacher in earlier years, but needs to remain an open discussion between teacher and pupils. Even the most well-planned motivation may still leave a few pupils unstimulated. These pupils will require more direct individual help and contextual clues from the teacher.

Subjects for drawing stem from several different types of pupil thinking and pupil experiences. Although their drawings differ in quality, most young artists can draw familiar objects. They reproduce details of what they have seen rather easily. This ability is called *visual memorization* or *visual recall*. Very young elementary age pupils employ scribbling as a form of *design* or *pattern*. This is often done for the pure enjoyment of the physical action. As pupils mature, they are able to draw *imaginary* subjects, applying their imagination to create original subjects. Many, but not all, pupils enjoy drawing from *direct observation* such as sketching outdoors or from pupil models in the classroom.

Beware of teaching drawing too formally. There is as much

"readiness" involved in drawing as there is in teaching reading. Correcting poor drawing ability can be inhibitive. Any common drawing faults can be explained to the total class carefully. Those pupils who become aware of their drawing errors will soon learn to correct these faults themselves.

Drawing Materials

Elementary school pupils should learn to draw using colored chalk, crayons, and a paint brush, as well as pen and ink. Using any combination of these drawing materials will add further variety and interest. Although large easel crayons are still necessary for young pupils lacking fine muscular control, children begin formal schooling today having had previous experiences with normal-size crayons and are able to use them successfully.

Try to avoid having pupils use pencils to draw and sketch. Using pencils to sketch subjects leads to many common drawing faults that are difficult to change later on in school life. The small, often finicky, details sketched in pencil are difficult to color. Coloring small details becomes a problem and frequently leads pupils away from using color more spontaneously. This is particularly true in using tempera or water-color paint to fill in pencil outlines.

There are many different kinds of paper and other surfaces available to draw upon, but the most common drawing material in most elementary schools is 54 lb.-weight manila paper. Manila paper is quite adequate for crayon drawings and is sold in several different sizes ranging from 9 × 12 inches to 18 × 24 inches. Various sizes of paper should be used to stimulate different drawings.

When colored chalk is used for drawing, a surface of contrasting-colored construction paper adds a "professional" touch. Use light-colored chalks against a black or purple background, or dark-colored chalks on a bright yellow or green background. Contrasting colors is a basic art principle that, when utilized, provides better results.

Occasionally, pupils should be motivated to draw larger or smaller than they normally do. Newsprint paper is the only inexpensive paper that is available in sizes as large as 24 × 36 inches. Pupils need to work on large pads of newspapers placed on the floor whenever they are using large-size paper. This change of size often stimulates different kinds of drawings.

Organization for Drawing

With the exception of creating murals, all drawing activities are individual and require no special classroom organization. The normal "rules" of having all materials readily available apply to all drawing activities. Some pupils tend to play with materials and are distracted from classroom discussion of a theme when materials are distributed prior to the discussion. Motivate first, then distribute materials immediately afterward.

Mural making requires a more complex classroom organization. After the theme for a mural has been selected and thoroughly discussed, pupils should select that part of the mural they would like to draw. Encourage the best artists to draw the more difficult subjects. As pupils complete the details of their part of the mural at their seats, they may be assigned a specific place to enlarge their drawing on the mural paper. There is room for all, including "touch-up" artists at the very end of the activity.

Common Problems in Drawing

The range in ability to visualize and draw is quite wide in most elementary classrooms. Younger pupils gradually develop their own schema, or symbols, for drawing people and common objects. These symbols for figures will vary from roughly drawn circles with feet and arms attached loosely to fully drawn heads and bodies, complete wtih five fingers illustrated on each hand. This wide span of visual ability should not be too disturbing to a teacher since, as in reading, practice and encouragement will improve drawing ability.

Some pupils are very visually perceptive, others are not. This is an excellent educational reason for exposing pupils to a great variety of drawing activities ranging from imaginary subjects to drawing from models. There are common drawing problems found in most elementary schools. Many of these problems can be lessened if analyzed properly by the teacher and discussed in a non-threatening manner with the class.

Younger pupils need more time to develop an emotional security about drawing; therefore their drawing activities should be based upon imaginary and creative motivations until drawing becomes a natural response. Older elementary pupils are capable of learning more of the elements of drawing through use of student models and drawing directly from observing nature.

Creativity is the philosophical thread that runs throughout the text of this book. How to motivate pupils to think for themselves, and to solve their own problems is emphasized in a practical manner that the classroom teacher can understand. There is no "Pie-in-the-Sky" approach here!

Note: The Guidelines in this and the following chapters are to guide your own thoughts as a teacher, and to offer suggestions for the conversations you will have with pupils before each activity begins.

DRAWING

DRAWING ACTIVITY (GRADE LEVEL)	NEW MATERIALS INTRODUCED	PHYSICAL SKILLS INVOLVED	PUPILS LEARN	EMOTIONAL AND INTELLECTUAL EXPERIENCES
What's in the Hole? (Using a hole for ideas) (2-6)		Cutting through paper to create a circular hole. Pushing scissors through paper.	To create new drawing ideas from strong stimuli. To elaborate upon an idea.	Selecting Discovering Imagining Deciding
Where's the Idea? (Ideas With Yarn) (2-6)	Cotton Roving or Jumbo Weight Yarn Chalk Fixatif	Spraying Using Side Chalk Gluing small objects.	To use the side of chalk to color large areas. To use fixatif.	Experimenting Exploring Ideas Visualizing
Inventing Your Own Machine (Detailed machine drawing) (2-6)	Pencil Drawing	Drawing small details using a pencil.	To draw a sequence of ideas. To use their imagination. To invent.	Inventing Detailing Imagining
Watch the Lines Flow (Ink and Wet Paper) (5-6)	Wet Paper Fine-pointed Pens	Drawing quickly. Drawing with a straight pen point.	To use different kinds of drawing tools. That drawing lines have texture.	Trying Out Working Spontaneously.
Drawing a Sound Story (sounds as stimuli) (3-6)	Cassette Tape Recorder/ Player	Taping and Timing Sounds	To create a drawing-sequence. To draw from a variety of stimuli.	Listening Creating Originating
Finding Every Edge (Using a framer) (5-6)	A framer	Drawing small details	To observe details. To draw parts of an object. The fundamentals of composition.	Observing Detailing Deciding Selecting Composing
Half-Animal, Half What? (Animal rearrangements) (4-6)		Drawing	To synthesize ideas. To create new arrangements.	Originating Synthesizing Creating Visualizing
Add to the Photographs (4-6)	Magazine Photographs	Pasting and drawing small details.	To elaborate upon an idea.	Elaborating Trying Out Relating Ideas
That Reminds Me of Something (Abstract Ideas) (2-6)	Free-Form Paper Shapes	Pasting Drawing details	To relate and associate abstract shapes to reality. To think originally.	Originating Elaborating Selecting Exploring Ideas

Objectives:

1. To learn to use imagination in selecting different subjects to draw.

2. To develop experience and ability to draw a variety of objects.

Materials:

18 × 24-inch manila paper or newsprint, colored crayons, small round objects to trace (dishes, paper cups, glasses), pencil.

Guidelines:

Tired of drawing the same old things over and over again? Why not force yourself to draw different subjects by cutting a hole in your drawing paper first . . . before you start thinking. Try not to think about any ideas as you trace around a circular object on paper and cut out the center of the traced circle. You will find ideas come easily as you begin to discuss different kinds of holes.

What kinds of holes can you think of? There are all kinds! There are holes left in doughnuts by the baker, holes that animals hide in and knotholes in fences to peek through. Which one will make the best subject for your drawing?

The hole already cut in your paper is going to influence your drawing. If you thought of using your hole as an animal's lair, where, on the paper, are you going to draw the animal? Scurrying to the hole, no doubt, since there is no paper left to show him inside his lair. Perhaps you have a family of groundhogs and will need to draw several circles to cut out.

Whatever idea you have selected should be drawn completely with one single-colored crayon. Black or brown crayons are the best crayons for sketching ideas. It is important to sketch all of your idea on paper first before you begin to add details in color. Fill the paper! Draw in the objects in the distance high up on your paper. Start those objects close to you at the bottom of the paper. This drawing habit will soon rid you of "base line" drawing and small disconnected drawing ideas.

How To Do It:

1. Use a pencil to trace a circular object on an 18 × 24-inch piece of manila paper (Figure 1-L1-2).

Figure 1-L1-1

2. Push the point of a closed pair of scissors through the center of the traced circle. Cut the center of the circle out of the background paper (Figure 1-L1-2).

Figure 1-L1-2

3. Discuss various ideas about holes with the class. Motivate ideas

and brainstorm with the group until the majority of pupils have individually different ideas they want to draw.

4. Use a black or brown crayon to sketch in details, the main idea and background in the drawing (Figure 1-L1-3).

Figure 1-L1-3

5. Add color with crayons to the completed drawing.

6. Clean up! Throw away scraps. Return glasses or objects used to trace the circles. Wash up!

Variations:

1. Repeat the activity using tempera paint or water colors. Pupils feel secure once they have learned a technique and tend to obtain ideas in less time, leaving more time for painting.

LESSON 2

Where's the Idea?

Objectives:

1. To learn about associative thinking.
2. To learn to use a variety of materials in drawing experiences.

Materials:

Heavyweight cotton roving or jumbo-weight yarn, clear spray fixatif, white glue or school paste, crayons, pencil, 12 × 18-inch colored construction paper, colored chalk, water cups, newspapers.

Guidelines:

An artist learns to see a whole picture from the shape of a line. You can teach yourself to use your imagination this way. (You don't have to study psychology in order to understand Gestalts.) Everyone thinks visually. With a few pieces of thick cotton roving and a bit of white glue you are ready to visualize your own original subject from clues that only you can see. Add a few details with colored chalk.

Play around with the heavy yarn on colored construction paper a moment or two. Try placing a two-foot length of roving in various positions on the paper. Look at the roving and think. Does part of the line or shape that the yarn created remind you of something? Is that curve part of a tiger ready to spring, or is it the body of a salmon ready to leap the waterfall? You will see your own "thing" in the shape created by the roving and draw ideas within your own experiences. If ideas don't seem to leap out at you at first, try experimenting with the roving again. Maybe this time your idea will come up!

If you are using colored chalk for the first time, try tearing a small piece of paper to place under your fingers. Chalk can create quite a few smudges and messes that can ruin your drawing, unless you are exceptionally neat. Some of the colored chalk may have hard surfaces. Scrape these colors on a piece of old newspaper to remove the polished surface of the chalk. You can use the side of the chalk to color large areas in your drawing. You'll find it easier to hold the pieces of colored chalk in a watercolor cup where they can't roll off the desk.

Wipe your hands carefully after using white glue to adhere roving to the background paper or you'll encounter some difficulty using the chalk cleanly.

How to Do It:

1. Pre-cut brightly-colored jumbo-weight yarn or heavy cotton roving into two-foot lengths for each pupil. Place several different pieces of colored chalk into watercolor pans for each pupil, or partners, to share (Figure 1-L2-1).

2. Cover each working surface with newspapers. Distribute the chalk (in water cups), glue, yarn, and colored construction paper to each pupil.

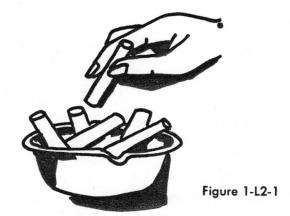

Figure 1-L2-1

3. Experiment with a variety of shapes and lines by manipulating the piece of yarn on colored construction paper until an idea is born. Select the idea that reminds you of a subject that you can draw with chalk. Trace lightly with a pencil around the line or shape created by the yarn to mark its position (Figure 1-L2-2).

Figure 1-L2-2

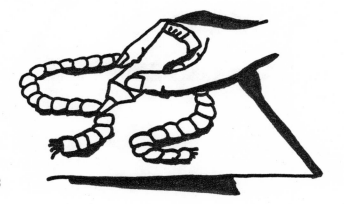

Figure 1-L2-3

4. Apply white glue to the surface of the yarn by using your finger or a tube of glue. Press the yarn into position over the traced line (Figure 1-L2-3).

5. Wipe off excess glue from hands.

6. Tear a small square of newspaper to use as a "holding paper" when drawing with chalk (Figure 1-L2-4).

Figure 1-L2-4

7. Use colored chalk to complete a drawing around the roving or yarn. Add details to the main subject using the point of the chalk. Use the side of the colored chalk to color large areas of the drawing. Spraying chalk with fixatif is optional (Figure 1-L2-5).

Figure 1-L2-5

8. Clean up by throwing away newspapers and scrap paper. Return excess glue to containers. Return chalk to boxes and wash hands before handling the finished drawing.

Variations:

1. Crayon and manila paper may be used in lieu of chalk and construction paper. Make sure that children draw in details fairly completely before beginning the final phase of coloring.

LESSON 3

Inventing Your Own Machine

Objectives:

1. To develop an attitude toward originality and inventiveness.
2. To learn to draw a variety of objects.

Materials:

Pencil, 12 × 18-inch manila paper.

Guidelines:

Inventiveness is what makes progress possible. The earlier it is developed, the better! Here's your chance to become as original an inventor as Thomas Edison or Benjamin Franklin.

Inventing machines is not so hard. All you need is an unusual problem and the rules by which the problem can be solved. How about inventing an apple-pie baking machine? A machine that actually goes right into the apple orchard and performs all the steps necessary to bake an apple pie! Think of all the operations! Picking the apples from the tree, coring, peeling and slicing the apples, adding spices and making a crust. What an opportunity to exercise your imagination!

There are plenty of problems to solve. How are the ingredients of the pie to be carried throughout the process? What sort of machine picks apples from trees? How are the ingredients mixed together? Where can you locate the oven to bake the pie? Your machine can be as complicated, or as simple, as you want to make it.

If you don't care about making apple pie, how about inventing a tomato-soup machine? One machine that can perform all of the steps to make soup right in the garden. What problems will you encounter? How can you peel the skins? What crushes, or strains, the peeled tomatoes? What else is used in tomato soup besides tomatoes? How can you get the soup into cans? Here are plenty of questions and problems to use your imagination on!

Perhaps a popcorn machine is too easy! How about a potato-chip machine? Can you invent a single, self-propelled, potato-chip machine that digs up the potatoes, peels them, removes the "eyes" and slices the potato thin enough to cook in oil? What parts of machines will be useful to know about? What machines help you move the potato slices to the boiling pot of oil? How are the potato chips packaged?

Inventing machines is fun and will make you think about things you never have thought about before. This is one of the few activities in which drawing with a pencil should be encouraged because of the many small, necessary details in the drawing.

How to Do It:

1. Select one of the suggested problems about invention and motivate discussion about the various steps and processes.

2. Ask leading questions of the class. Use contextual clues in the discussion whenever necessary.

Figure 1-L3-1

3. Pass out pieces of 12 × 18-inch manila paper to each pupil.

4. Have each pupil draw an unusual machine. Everyone should print the titles of the various parts on his drawing (Figure 1-L3-1).

5. Clean up by storing drawings and washing up.

Variations:

1. Use colored crayons or any other familiar drawing media for a follow-up activity on much larger paper.

2. Several groups can work together inventing a more complicated machine.

LESSON 4
Watch the Lines Flow

Objectives:

1. To learn to draw using a variety of instruments.

2. To experience the visual impact of different types of drawing lines.

Materials:

Fine pen points and pen holder, 12 × 18-inch white painting paper, water cups, small bottles of black drawing ink, cellulose sponges, newspaper, Kleenex tissues.

Guidelines:

A little dampness on paper will ordinarily ruin your drawing and create havoc in general. But not if you learn to control it! Drawing can be more fun if different drawing tools are used. Limiting yourself to drawing merely with pencil or crayon may hinder your spontaneity and also prove a barrier to learning about different kinds of drawing lines. Drawing with fine pen points is a new experience.

A damp paper surface produces a beautiful, feathery drawing

line—a soft edge. If you ever have tried to imitate the soft edge of a flower petal, or the changing edge of a cloud on a sunny day, you have encountered the difficulty of mastering a feathery line texture. Your problems are solved, for a little dampness will automatically help your drawing turn into a feathery line.

Too much water on the paper's surface creates another problem, that of too much flowing, making your drawing line disappear on the surface. This can be avoided by testing the damp surface of the paper with pen and ink. If your drawing line feathers out and disappears quickly, the paper surface is still too wet to work upon. Wait a while and test the surface again. Some papers absorb water more quickly than others, so testing your line is always necessary.

Almost any subject is possible with this drawing technique, but simple subjects like flowers, boats and trees are particularly interesting since the soft edge of line helps to create a form of "impressionism."

How to Do It:

1. Prepare for pen and ink drawing by spreading newspapers to protect desks. Distribute water, water cups, white painting paper, drawing ink, pens and pen points and Kleenex tissues to each pupil.

2. Spread water evenly over the entire surface of a piece of white painting paper using a cellulose sponge (Figure 1-L4-1).

Figure 1-L4-1

3. Use pads of Kleenex tissues to absorb any excess pools of water that form on the surface of the paper (Figure 1-L4-2).

4. Dip the pen point into the small bottle of ink and remove excess ink by rubbing the pen point across the mouth of the ink bottle (Figure 1-L4-3).

5. Test the ink line on the wet surface of the paper to test the line.

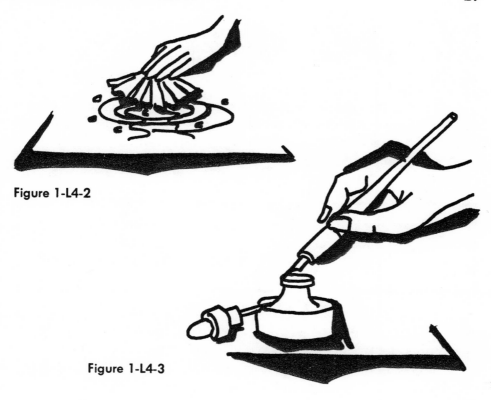

Figure 1-L4-2

Figure 1-L4-3

6. Draw your subject quickly before the dampness of the paper dries and the flowing line is lost (Figure 1-L4-4).

Figure 1-L4-4

7. Clean up by wiping off each pen point with a damp cloth.

Empty water cups into the sink, squeeze out sponges and throw away used Kleenex tissues. Place the damp drawing to dry and wash up.

Variations:

1. Use a Magic Marker on the wet paper surface in lieu of pen and ink. Color may be added to the drawing more easily if Magic Markers are used.

LESSON 5

Drawing a Sound Story

Objectives:

1. To learn to use a variety of subjects and motivations for drawing.

2. To develop and reinforce individual thinking and imagination.

Materials:

Tape recorder, a selection of pre-taped sounds, crayons, 12 × 18-inch manila paper.

Guidelines:

If you own, or can borrow, a small cassette tape recorder you are ready to begin one of the most exciting drawing activities imaginable. Creating from taped sounds stimulates each imagination differently. Who knows what a series of sounds will make you think of? Your friend across the way seemed to hear and think about something entirely different!

Don't worry about which sounds to tape, they're all around you. The strongest sound motivations are animal noises. Start listening and taping sounds of barking dogs, yowling cats or any loud birds you may have hanging around outside the house. Don't overlook great, loud noises such as fire engines, loud explosions or squeaking doors in your own home. Perhaps those squeaking doors in the house may come in handy after all.

The sounds that you tape need not tell a story but should be related in some way. Some great Hallowe'en drawing can stem from motivations that include a squealing cat, squeaky doors, thuds of falling bodies and ghostly moans. Make up your own sequences for various occasions! If you plan ahead far enough, you may be able to copy sounds from the sound records at your local radio station. They have great collections of recorded sounds.

Play the sounds through once for listening, a second time for thinking. It takes time to incubate ideas and think about how the sounds apply to a drawing.

How to Do It:

1. Pre-tape a sequence of four or five sounds on a small cassette player-recorder (Figure 1-L5-1).

Figure 1-L5-1

2. Distribute crayons and a 12 × 18-inch manila paper to each pupil.

3. Play the sequence of taped sounds to the class without explaining the activity.

4. Explain the drawing activity to the class and repeat playing the sounds (Figure 1-L5-2).

Figure 1-L5-2

5. Use a brown crayon to lightly sketch out the drawing on manila paper.

6. Complete the drawing using colored crayons (Figure 1-L5-3).

Figure 1-L5-3

7. Clean up by storing the crayons and washing up. Rewind the cassette tape for future use.

Variations:

1. Use different sound sequences or encourage pupils to tape sounds themselves in the school or at home. Let them "borrow" or use their own tape recorders to think out their own combination of sounds.

LESSON 6

Finding Every Edge

Objectives:

1. To learn about composing and arranging elements in a drawing.

2. To learn to draw from direct observation.

Materials:

Black Magic Markers, or black crayons, 12 × 18-inch manila paper, 35mm slide mounts with the film removed, pads of newspapers.

Guidelines:

Looking around for something to draw? You're in the middle of an unlimited number of ideas right in your classroom. All you need to motivate drawing all these subjects is a different way of "looking at things."

Use a sharp single-edge razor blade to carefully remove the film from the center of any old 35mm slides and you have created a viewer than can lead to finding many different drawings. Ideas are all around you, it just requires a little different look. Practice the act of observing through the 35 millimeter frame you have created. Did you observe that the "picture" looked better when the bird cage was in the upper right hand corner, rather than the center, of the frame? Wasn't it better visually when part of the chair in the lower part of the "picture" was cut off and not shown? These are just a few of the things you may discover when you use a view finder to think about what you want to draw.

Learn to draw part of an object, not all of it. Beginning artists seldom draw half of an object but usually draw all of an object in their drawings. Beginners tend to draw "what they know" rather than "what they see." Observing that objects can look real when only part of the object is shown in a drawing is an important big step. Your view finder can help you find out this truth by yourself and this is usually the most exciting way to find out about new concepts.

If you haven't been drawing much recently, it may "pay" to warm up the rusty drawing activities prior to beginning this activity. Security is the basis of drawing, much the same as it is in academic areas.

How to Do It:

1. Use a single-edge razor blade to remove the film from 35 millimeter slide frames prior to the lesson (Figure 1-L6-1).

2. Distribute drawing paper, crayons, and view finders to each pupil.

3. Look through the view finder to locate an interesting drawing subject. Note that some objects are not completely within the framed picture. Only parts of these objects are visible (Figure 1-L6-2).

Figure 1-L6-1

Figure 1-L6-2

4. Use a black crayon to sketch out the complete drawing (Figure 1-L6-3).

Figure 1-L6-3

5. Complete the drawing by filling in details, using the same black crayon.

6. Clean up by saving the view finders for future activities and wash up.

Variations:

1. Cut your own view finder from cardboard or take the view finder outdoors after experiencing an indoor drawing activity.

LESSON 7

Half Animal—Half What?

Objectives:

1. To stimulate original thinking.

2. To learn to associate several drawing ideas into new combinations.

Materials:

Black, orange and red crayons, 18 × 24-inch newsprint or manila paper, pads of newspapers.

Guidelines:

New drawing ideas frequently stem from thinking about new combinations of old ideas. Time tells us that ideas for drawings are unlimited, but ideas are also highly dependent upon what the individual brain already has stored and memorized. Start storing ideas!

Begin by thinking about animal characteristics, the wilder the characteristics the better! How about a giraffe with his long neck, horns and spots? Suppose this giraffe were drawn in combination with a mouse with its round ears, small body and long tail. What would the result be? A new animal, of course! But, which particular physical characteristics of these animals would you combine to create your new animal? There are several problems to think about. Will the colors of the animals be different? Shall the animals be divided in half equally, or can their different characteristics be drawn together in some weird combination?

Since animals with very strong physical characteristics are the easiest to draw, start thinking about animals such as a rhinoceros, with his long tusk and short, fat body; the flat-tailed beaver; lions; etc. Make two lists of as many different animals as you can think of! Select an animal from each list that you create. Try to select two very different kinds of animals so that your new combination of the two animals will be very different.

Sketch lightly—you may want to draw over some of your first ideas and thoughts. It is easy to color and draw over lines if you sketch out your ideas lightly, using a brown or orange crayon.

How to Do It:

1. Distribute crayons and paper to each pupil. Place several layers of newspaper as pads under the drawing paper.

2. Discuss the physical characteristics of various animals stressing their differences. Use pupil responses to create two lists of animals on the blackboard.

3. Select two very different animals from the list to draw.

4. Use a brown or orange crayon to sketch out lightly the combination of the two animals selected (Figure 1-L7-1).

5. Add details to the drawing (Figure 1-L7-2).

LION - RABBIT

Figure 1-L7-1

Figure 1-L7-2

6. Clean up by washing up and passing the waste paper basket.

Variations:

1. Use birds and animal combinations instead of two animals. Repeat the lesson and concentrate upon color using tempera paint. Students already familiar with thinking about combinations will be able to introduce color more easily to their ideas.

LESSON 8

Add to the Photograph!

Objectives:

1. To learn to create a drawing using a photograph as the central subject and motivation.

2. To learn how to expand an idea and add drawing details to a subject.

Materials:

A magazine photograph, scissors, paste, black crayon, 18 × 24-inch or 12 × 18-inch manila drawing paper, newspapers, Kleenex tissues.

Guidelines:

Magazines lying around the house are a gold mine for stimulating different ideas. Have you been drawing the same old thing every time? Now's the time to be different! We all tend to rely upon familiar ideas. This is a good chance to change and begin thinking about drawing different subjects. It's easy! The idea is already in front of you in the form of a magazine picture!

Some magazines contain a wealth of pictures, several on every page. Selecting pictures from all those available on the pages need not present a problem. Don't think, just cut! Since you're looking for different ideas, cut out anything, from a picture of a fork in a silverware advertisement to a surfboard rider. Who knows which photograph will stimulate the best idea for any individual?

How about using the element of surprise? If you place the photographs face down on the desks, you won't have to worry about which photograph to use. Just pick one up and begin!

Which photograph did you get? A picture of an airplane? What ideas did it stimulate? An airport? An airplane in flight, or perhaps mechanics working on the airplane? Use a black crayon to develop ideas related to the pasted photograph. Some ideas may be large; better use the largest-size paper you have available. Did that large photograph of a fork stump you? Stop to think! What is the fork lifting? Who is holding it? Perhaps the fork is rolling up strands of spaghetti. Add a little imagination and start drawing.

Use only one colored crayon to complete the drawing. Don't worry about color, just draw and you'll end up with your own different idea—one that you've probably never used before.

How to Do It:

1. Cut out a variety of photographs from magazines prior to the activity. Actually cut out objects *from* the photographs, not just the perimeter of a photograph (Figure 1-L8-1).

Figure 1-L8-1

2. Distribute newspapers, black crayons, paste, manila paper, and paper towels to each pupil.

3. Pass out magazine photographs face down to each individual at random.

4. Experiment before pasting the photograph in place on the background paper (Figure 1-L8-2).

Figure 1-L8-2

5. Use a black crayon to add details, figures and background to complete the drawing (Figure 1-L8-3).

Figure 1-L8-3

6. Clean up and save the remaining paste. Wash up! Save surplus illustrations for future decoupage activities.

Variations:

1. Encourage pupils to find their own photographic illustrations at home and bring them to school. Use a complete set of colored crayons to add color to the picture.

That Reminds Me of Something!

Objectives:

1. To learn to use abstract shapes to create realistic drawings.
2. To develop the use of imagination.

Materials:

A variety of pre-cut abstract shapes from colored paper, colored crayons, paste, 12 × 18-inch manila paper, newspapers.

Guidelines:

Once in a while you need to draw something totally different, something more challenging than the ordinary. Most drawing ideas stem from memory or observation. Why not begin a drawing lesson without any idea at all? Let the idea be born later, motivated and stimulated by an abstract shape.

The scientists who pioneered in the field of Gestalt psychology left many ideas for future artists. Almost everyone has visual imagination to "see" some real subject in a non-objective shape. Sometimes an idea is stimulated by the color or the paper used. Sometimes it is the lyrical curve of a cut-paper shape that establishes an idea in the eye of the beholder. Using abstract or non-objective shapes works because everyone thinks individually and differently.

Cut a variety of free-form shapes directly from colored paper. Select each shape randomly so that no one has a choice, or time to select a specific shape. Start looking closely for something "real" in the abstract form.

Does that particular shape remind you of a teardrop? Think about what you must add to the shape to create a drawing with a teardrop. An eye? A face? A sad thing?

What does that elongated orange piece of paper remind you of? A hot dog roll, wings of an old World War I airplane or perhaps a hat for a bullfighter? Who knows? Your imagination is your own!

Can't think of an idea? Why not turn the abstract paper shape upside down and begin thinking again? Try placing the Gestalt shape in various locations on the paper; perhaps it looks more realistic to you when it is in the middle of the paper, or in the corner.

How to Do It:

1. Pre-cut a variety of colored-paper shapes prior to the drawing activity. Use several different colors and free-form shapes to avoid duplication of ideas (Figure 1-L9-1).

Figure 1-L9-1

2. Cover each desk with newspapers and distribute 12 × 18-inch manila paper, paste, colored crayons, and the pre-cut paper shapes to each pupil.

3. Experiment placing the abstract paper shape in various locations on the manila paper, turn it upside down, try it in various positions. Think about what the shape reminds you of.

4. Paste the paper shape into the desired location on the manila paper (Figure 1-L9-2).

PASTE

Figure 1-L9-2

5. Once the subject has been decided, use colored crayons to add details to the paper shape, making it a real subject or object (Figure 1-L9-3).

Figure 1-L9-3

6. Clean up by saving paste, excess colored-paper scraps and store newspapers and crayons. Wash up!

Variations:

1. Use tempera paint instead of crayons to complete the idea after pupils have already experienced the basic concept of developing realistic ideas from abstract shapes.

CHAPTER **2**

Using Crayons Many Ways

INTRODUCTION TO CRAYONS

Wax crayons are probably the most common art medium used in elementary schools today. They are easy to handle, add color to pictures quickly and are simple to store. Many young children have experienced using crayons before they began formal schooling, and feel secure with the medium. This security makes crayons the best beginning art media to explore creatively with.

Crayons may be used in many different ways, ranging from melted crayon candles and simple "batik" wax patterns on cloth, to just plain drawing. Even drawing activities with wax crayons can be varied sufficiently to add new interest to this underrated art medium. Crayons may be used to draw on cloth, wood, paper, rocks and even on sandpaper. Each drawing surface combines with crayon to produce its own individual texture that is different from all others. The side of a wax crayon may be used to add soft color to large areas of a drawing. The texture of side crayon differs from the intense line produced when the point of a crayon is used.

Light-colored crayons, such as brown or orange, should be used to sketch and outline subjects in a drawing before coloring. These light-colored sketching lines are easily covered over with other colors when color is added to the drawing.

Work with crayons is basic to young children's art and, therefore, deserves time and planning.

Crayon Materials

Crayons are the least complex of all materials used in elementary school. Each pupil should store his own individual set of crayons to keep and maintain. If crayons are purchased in bulk instead of as individual sets of colors, the loose crayons may be kept in metal Band-Aid cans or simply held together with a rubber band. Eight colors—yellow, orange, red, green, blue, brown, purple and black —constitute all the colors a pupil will need. The fewer colors the better, as pupils will be forced to "mix" their own different colors on the paper rather than merely picking up the "right" color.

Whenever crayons are used for drawing purposes, a "bed" of newspapers should be placed underneath the drawing paper. Without this soft "bed," crayons tend to produce an unattractively hard, waxy line texture.

Organizing for Crayon Activities

Most crayon lessons are individual activities that require no complex organizational pattern. All individually-based crayon lessons follow a sequence of: (1) discussion of the activity, its subject or theme; (2) any demonstration of new techniques or materials; (3) distribution of materials; (4) the crayon activity and (5) cleanup and storage of materials.

Group activities using crayons, such as candle making, batiking and crayon etchings require moving desks together to create a larger working surface area for the many additional materials that need to be shared by pupils.

A scrap-crayon box should be located in a corner of the room and pupils should be encouraged to "trade in" stubby, worn-out crayons for new ones. At the end of the year, this scrap-crayon material can be used in a variety of different ways.

Common Problems in Crayon Activities

There are fewer opportunities for error in using crayons than in other art activities. Some pupils may encounter difficulty coloring over their drawing lines because they tend to press too hard with their "drawing" crayon. These pupils need to be encouraged to sketch more lightly.

Frequently, pupils supplement school crayons with their own crayons. Crayons purchased in department stores are seldom of the same high quality as school crayons, even though the manufacturer's label may be the same. Lesser quality crayons leave a waxy residue on the paper surface and frequently are less intense in color. When you observe residues or weak color, persuade pupils to substitute school crayons for the commercial crayons in order to maintain quality in both color and line.

Wax crayons are frequently used in "resist" type art activities such as batik and crayon resist. Pupils should be sure that the crayon actually will resist any paint by first sketching lightly, then tracing over the crayon lines, pressing more firmly on the crayon.

It is normal for children to want to correct any errors or whatever they think they have drawn poorly. However, this sometimes constitutes a problem when the drawing is done with a wax crayon. Attempting to erase a crayon line usually results only in a smear on the paper. Pupils should be encouraged to sketch lightly and draw "over" their errors. When color is applied to the drawing, a dark-colored crayon will help to cover any errors.

CRAYONS

CRAYON ACTIVITY (GRADE LEVEL)	NEW MATERIALS INTRODUCED	PHYSICAL SKILLS INVOLVED	PUPILS LEARN	EMOTIONAL AND INTELLECTUAL EXPERIENCES
Finding What's Underneath (Crayon Etching) (2-4)	Oak Tag Liquid Soap Scrapers (scissors)	Scraping with tools to remove top surface.	To use color randomly. To draw with different tools.	Trying Out Deciding Finding
Rubbing It On (Crayon Rubbing) (3-6)	Textured Surfaces Side crayons	Pulling crayons across a surface.	To use the side of the crayon for creating large colored areas.	Trying Out Selecting Discovering
Using All of the Crayon (Side Crayon) (2-3)		Pulling crayons across surfaces.	To use crayons in different ways.	Arranging Composing Finding
Wax Crayon Candles (5-6)	Heated Crayon Paper Cupcake Forms	Pouring hot wax. Forming wicks and wick holders.	That crayons flow and can be cast into forms. To create a functional object.	Experimenting Discovering
Crayoning Cloth (Crayon designs on Cotton) (3-4)	Muslin or Cotton Cloth Iron	Using crayon on a limp surface. Ironing cloth. Transferring designs.	To repeat designs and subjects. To create a functional art object.	Touching Trying Out Deciding
Crumple Paper into Leather (Crumpled Paper Designs) (4-6)	Brown Wrapping Paper Colored Inks Pins	Crumpling paper into a ball. Pinning paper to a pad.	That some designs are created naturally and accidentally.	Discovering
Sliding the Paint Over (Crayon Resist with Watercolors) (3-6)	Watercolor Boxes	Mixing larger amounts of color. Painting with long, even strokes.	To mix large amounts of color. To use long brush strokes to fill background.	Discovering Visualizing

Finding What's Underneath!

Objectives:

1. To learn crayon etching techniques.
2. To learn to use imagination when thinking about ideas.

Materials:

Black tempera paint, liquid soap, crayons, oak tag (9 × 12 inches), watercolor brushes (size 12 preferred), watercolor cups, masking tape, scissors or stencil knives, newspapers.

Guidelines:

Usually, crayon etchings are produced by rubbing soft, black wax crayons over other crayon colors, then etching through the black crayon surface to the color below. This can be a long, tiring process. Looking for a shortcut? This is your answer! You can accomplish the same result more easily by using tempera paint and soap, and you won't have to wait as long to get at the drawing phase of the activity.

Color away to your heart's content with crayons on a piece of heavy oak tag. Use bright-colored crayons to cover the oak tag with stripes, random shapes, or even plaids. Cover with the mixture of soap and black tempera. After you scrape through the painted surface, the bright colors will contrast noticeably. Covering the crayon surface of the oak tag with the paint mixture saves time but it causes the oak tag to curl. You can compensate for this curling by using masking tape to hold down the corners of the oak tag to the newspaper. Pins will also do the job!

Liquid soap mixes well with tempera paint to cover the waxy crayon surface. After the crayon surface is covered with paint and soap, you'll probably have to wait about ten minutes for the surface to dry.

Use this time to incubate ideas! What shall we etch—butterflies, underwater scenes, a farm, or perhaps even just a design? Once you are ready with your idea, pick up a closed pair of scissors or stencil knife and start drawing on the oak tag. The more color that you remove, the more colorful your picture will be. Use the side of your scissors to remove more color!

How to Do It:

1. Add an ounce or two of liquid soap to a quart of black tempera paint and mix the two ingredients thoroughly. Pre-cut pieces of heavy weight oak tag into 9 × 12-inch pieces.

2. Distribute newspapers to cover desks. Each pupil will need: a large watercolor brush, a piece of oak tag, four strips of masking tape, a pair of scissors (or stencil knife) and a watercolor cup partially filled with the soap and paint mixture.

3. Cover the entire surface of the oak tag with color by using soft wax crayons. Use any color pattern you wish but cover all of thé surface pressing heavily on the crayons (Figure 2-L1-1).

Figure 2-L1-1

Figure 2-L1-2

4. Dip the large watercolor brush into the black paint and soap mixture, allowing a liberal amount of paint to flow over the crayoned surface. Brush this mixture over the wax crayon surface until the entire surface is covered (Figure 2-L1-2).

5. It will take a few minutes for the paint to dry. Take this time to thoroughly discuss and motivate subjects.

6. Use a closed pair of scissors, or a stencil knife, to draw through the painted surface exposing the crayon colors below (Figure 2-L1-3).

Figure 2-L1-3

7. Use the blade of the scissors, or any other sharp flat tool, to remove large areas of paint (Figure 2-L1-4).

Figure 2-L1-4

8. Brush paint and excess wax away. Remove the masking tape that held the etching to the newspapers.

9. Use the scissors to round corners on the oak tag to eliminate the areas covered by the masking tape.

10. Clean up by brushing wax bits onto newspapers, wash out paint brushes and water cups under cold water. Throw away newspapers. Return crayons and other materials to their proper locations and wash up!

Variations:

1. Cut out small colored photographs from magazines and paste them in overlapping positions on the surface of the etching, leaving some spaces open for the colorful background.

2. Change the subject of the etching. Use underwater or city scenes as the theme.

LESSON 2

Rubbing It On!

Objectives:

1. To learn to use the side of a crayon to add color to large surface areas.

2. To learn about the process of reproducing textures by rubbings.

Materials:

Aluminum screening or small-diameter chicken wire cut into small pieces, soft wax crayons, newsprint paper, pads of newspapers.

Guidelines:

Every now and then we all like to rub it in a little! Don't pass over this opportunity to use crayons and textural materials to reproduce textures through rubbing. Rubbing is such a simple activity that you may tend to look down upon it at first, until you give a little more thought to the unlimited possibilities it offers.

Tombstone rubbings are a traditional project, but why should rubbings be limited to grave stones? Surely there are more interesting textures than grave stones to explore. You may be the one to find these surfaces. Any strong texture that lies flat and will fit underneath a piece of newsprint can be used for a rubbing. You'll find chicken wire, screening and some plastic surfaces the most common objects to find and collect. But there are a number of other materials you can use for crayon rubbings. Test each new material by rubbing a peeled crayon over paper placed over its surface. If it reproduces the texture evenly, the surface is functional for a rubbing.

Completing your rubbing is only the beginning. Begin thinking about subjects and ideas you're going to draw over the rubbed background. Does that rubbing made over aluminum screening remind you of a fence? Perhaps you can draw figures in a schoolyard or an airport over the texture.

Those squares produced by rubbing crayon over chicken wire look like windows. What's behind those windows? Start thinking about your drawing ideas while you're rubbing. Let those ideas germinate a little and you'll be ready to fill the paper with more than just the rubbing textures!

How to Do It:

1. Collect textures that can be used for rubbing and cut the material into functional sizes (Figure 2-L2-1).

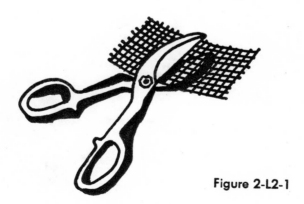

Figure 2-L2-1

2. Peel the paper from a crayon to rub over the texture (brown, orange, or green are good medium colors). Distribute pads of newspapers, crayons, pre-cut material for rubbing and newsprint to each pupil.

3. Place the textured material over the thick pad of newspapers. Add a piece of newsprint over the material (Figure 2-L2-2).

Figure 2-L2-2

4. Place the peeled crayon flat on the surface of the newsprint. Without lifting any part of the crayon from the surface, *pull* the crayon completely across the surface of the paper pressing down heavily on the crayon. Repeat this action until the surface is completely filled by the rubbing (Figure 2-L2-3).

5. Use bright-colored crayons to draw your ideas over the rubbed background (Figure 2-L2-4).

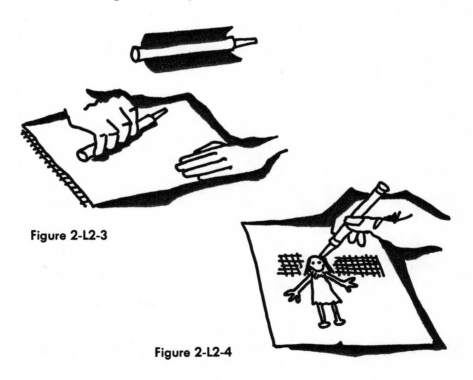

Figure 2-L2-3

Figure 2-L2-4

6. Clean up by using paper towels to clean desks, throw away newspapers, and save the scrap materials for collages. Wash up!

Variations:

1. Vary the activity by using different textures underneath mini-pieces of paper. Add small drawings to the backgrounds.

2. Use a combination of textures as a background and draw a design over the rubbed surface.

LESSON 3

Using All of the Crayon!

Objectives:

1. To learn different techniques with crayons.

2. To learn to create background areas quickly by using a side crayon technique.

Materials:

Soft wax crayons; a stack of newspapers for every pupil; manila or white paper.

Guidelines:

Have you been using only the point of a wax crayon to produce your masterpieces? You'll soon find out that there are other parts of your crayons that also are useful. Why not try peeling the paper from that purple crayon and using the side of it to produce colorful backgrounds for your designs or drawings? Using the side of the crayon is certainly not a new technique, but it may be an overlooked one. Sides of the crayon create a different texture from the points, and this difference can be useful.

Need a soft blue color in your drawing for the sky or expanse of ocean? Why waste effort and time coloring away with the point of your crayon? Try the side of the crayon and cover the "whole thing" in a brief period of time. Side crayon techniques result in a soft shaded texture that varies greatly from the texture produced when the point of the crayon is used.

Whole skies can become reality with a few pulls of a crayon across the paper. Smaller details can be easily added over this background color, particularly if the crayons are darker colors. Need a few trees to overlap your sky? Break off a small piece of that brown crayon, place it flat on the paper, and pull! One thing you'll need to be successful is a thick pad of newspapers underneath your drawing paper. This pliant pad of newspaper provides the soft foundation that is necessary to produce the soft texture characteristic of side crayon.

How to Do It:

1. Distribute a stack of newspapers, crayons and a 12″ × 18″-piece of manilla paper to each pupil. Arrange the newspapers on the desk to provide a thick base for the manila paper. Peel the paper from a brown crayon (Figure 2-L3-1).

Figure 2-L3-1

2. Use the point of the crayon to sketch only the background areas of a landscape or seascape. Concentrate upon sketching the background and avoid adding details (Figure 2-L3-2).

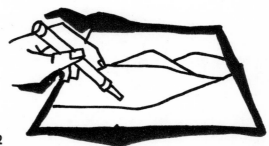

Figure 2-L3-2

3. Place a crayon so that it lies flat upon the manila paper. Using

one hand to hold down the paper, apply pressure to the peeled crayon as it is *pulled toward* you (Figure 2-L3-3).

Figure 2-L3-3

4. Repeat this pulling action until all of the background areas have been covered using different colors of crayons.

5. Use the point of a crayon to draw and color foreground details (Figure 2-L3-4).

Figure 2-L3-4

6. Clean up by collecting and stacking the newspapers. Return small scraps of crayon to the scrap box and wash up.

Variations:

1. Use side crayon techniques to create a random design and draw another design over this, using the point of the crayon.

Wax Crayon Candles!

Objectives:

1. To learn to create functional objects using wax crayons.
2. To develop skills and craftsmanship in working with wax.

Materials:

Scrap wax crayons, old double-boiling pots, a stove or portable heating element, paraffin, small paper bake cups, candle wicking, scissors, a small piece of clay, toothpicks or lollipop sticks, newspapers.

Guidelines:

You may never be able to burn these candles at both ends, but making them will certainly be fun. All you need is some paraffin that can be obtained at your local supermarket or gas station (wax is a by-product of petroleum). The color of your candle is limited to whatever scrap wax crayons you have on hand to add to the melted wax.

Melting the wax crayons and paraffin together calls for both a stove and a double boiler. Never attempt to melt paraffin in a pot directly over heat; it is flammable. Always place the container of wax in water and heat the water. A few pounds of paraffin will make up to 30 candles if you use small-size paper bake cups. If you desire larger candles, you will need more paraffin and more crayons. Rolls of candle wicking are inexpensive and can be obtained from any craft shop. You'll need only a few inches of wicking for each candle because bake cups are not very high. A bit of clay anchors the wicking to the bottom of the bake cups. Wicks need to be tied around a crosspiece to hold them upright in the mold. A lollipop stick or toothpick will do this.

Create a working area near your hotplate or stove. Cover this table liberally with newspapers in readiness for the pouring activity. If you have more than one double boiler to spare, you can pour a candle in layers of two different colors. Once you peel away the paper exterior, the layers of color will be displayed beautifully.

How to Do It:

1. Begin pre-heating paraffin in double boilers over a hotplate or stove. Use approximately a pound of wax for each eight candles. Stir and melt several crayons of one color in each pot. Adding more crayons will make a more intense color (Figure 2-L4-1).

Figure 2-L4-1

2. Distribute paper baking cups, small pieces of clay, five-inch lengths of candle wicking and scissors to each pupil.

3. Wrap and tie the wicking around a toothpick or lollipop stick (Figure 2-L4-2).

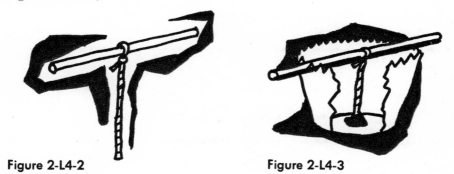

Figure 2-L4-2   **Figure 2-L4-3**

4. Anchor the length of candlewicking at the bottom of the baking cup by wrapping one end of the wicking in clay as illustrated in the cutaway view (Figure 2-L4-3).

5. Carry the completed paper bake cup mold to the double boiler. Pour the molten crayon mixture into the mold (Figure 2-L4-4).

Figure 2-L4-4

6. Clean up by scraping excess old wax from the double boilers and scour the interior of the pot with cleansing powder and a stiff brush. Return broken crayons to the scrap box and salvage any left-over materials. Wash up!

Variations:

1. Use two double boiling pots and pour layers of alternating color, allowing each layer of color to harden before pouring the next.

2. Apply heat to each candle and join several candles together to create a group of candles.

LESSON 5

Crayoning Cloth

Objectives:

1. To learn to use crayons on different surfaces.

2. To become aware of the concept of repetition as an element of design.

Materials:

Cotton or muslin cloth, wax crayons, scissors, manila paper, an electric iron, soft graphite pencils, newspapers.

Guidelines:

By this time you have probably found that crayons can be used on almost any type of surface or material: add cloth to this long list of materials.

Look around your house for an old pillowcase or piece of muslin. Since your design will provide all the color you'll need, why not select plain white cloth for the background? Cut pieces of your pillowcase into different sizes. No need to worry about exact shapes or dimensions unless you've already decided what you're going to make. If you've decided upon making a wall hanging, a small tablecloth or perhaps just a colorful book mark, size becomes more important.

Need a wall hanging to add a little brightness to your room? Get out those wax crayons and get started! Begin by sketching out your design on a piece of manila paper cut the same size as the cloth. Experiment with a design that follows the cloth border, or begin with a strong central design that spreads out radially to all areas of the paper. Polish your design a bit, add some details and you're ready to transfer it to the final piece of cloth. Once transferred you can add all the further details you want.

Rinse the completed design in cold water to eliminate any pencil smudges. It is necessary to "set" the wax crayon color into the fibers of the cloth with the heat of an electric iron. Never apply the hot iron directly to a waxed surface. Always place a sheet of newspaper between the wax and the hot iron as protection. Once your wax design is "set" into the cloth, it can be washed in cold water without much color loss.

How to Do It:

1. Distribute scissors, cloth, manila paper and newspapers to each pupil. Spread newspapers to protect the desks. Begin pre-heating an electric iron at a table located in the room.

2. Pre-cut pieces of white cotton cloth (or muslin) the same size as a piece of manila paper (Figure 2-L5-1).

3. Use a crayon to draw designs around the border of the manila paper or draw one large design that completely fills the paper (Figure 2-L5-2).

Figure 2-L5-1

Figure 2-L5-2

4. Rub the back of the completed design with a soft pencil. Fasten the manila paper and cloth together with paper clips placing the "penciled" side next to the cloth surface. Use a fairly sharp pencil to lightly transfer the image from the paper to the cloth (Figure 2-L5-3).

5. Using wax crayons, redraw the design on the cloth. Press heavily on the crayon (Figure 2-L5-4).

Figure 2-L5-3

Figure 2-L5-4

6. Carry the completed design to the sink and rinse it under water. Squeeze it dry. Place the cloth, crayon side down, on a stack of newspapers and cover it with a piece of paper. Iron this paper to "set" the crayon design into the cloth fiber (Figure 2-L5-5).

7. Clean up by throwing away small scraps and saving larger scraps for other lessons. Unplug the electric iron and store tools and materials. Wash up!

Figure 2-L5-5

Variations:

1. Sew or glue the design around two dowels to create a wall hanging or banner.

2. Paint cold water dyes on the design with a brush or sponge to make it more colorful.

LESSON 6

Crumple Paper into Leather

Objectives:

1. To introduce an elementary form of batik to younger students.

2. To develop an awareness of spontaneous design.

Materials:

Brown wrapping paper, brown wax crayons, pails of water, brown colored inks, pins, large brushes, plastic pails, newspapers.

Guidelines:

Like the alchemists of old who dreamed of making gold from lead you can create your own alchemy with just a few brown crayons, paper, and a few common pins. The process is a simple one. By drawing with crayons heavily on the surface of a brown paper bag or wrapping paper, you have a material that can be dampened, colored and crackled.

If you don't really "turn on" through the process of creating leather from brown paper bags and brown crayons, you can easily switch to any other colors and paper. Almost any heavy paper lacking a glossy surface can be substituted to create a crackled paper. Since the design you are working on is a "happening" that cannot be planned, it is not necessary to draw any specific subject. Use the crayon randomly, scribbling first with one colored crayon, then another. These random lines will be transformed drastically when colored inks, or watercolors, are washed over the damp paper. The slow drying out process will cause more crinkling of the paper and wax design. If you're in a hurry, you can accelerate the whole drying process by not using pins and ironing the back of the brown paper with an electric iron.

How to Do It:

1. Cover desks with thick pads of newspapers. Fill plastic pails with water. Distribute inks or watercolors, crayons, pins and large brushes to small groups of pupils to share.

2. Pre-cut and distribute pieces of brown wrapping paper, or other thick non-glossy paper, into desired shapes and sizes. These may range from 9 × 12 inches to 18 × 24 inches.

3. Pressing heavily upon a wax crayon, draw a line design filling the paper (Figure 2-L6-1).

Figure 2-L6-1

4. Dip the crayon design under water in a plastic pail. Crumple the paper into a ball, stretch it flat again and place it on a stack of newspapers, crayon side up (Figure 2-L6-2).

5. Use a large brush to coat the wet paper surface with colored ink or watercolor (Figure 2-L6-3).

6. Use common pins to hold the wet paper firmly to the pad of

Figure 2-L6-2

Figure 2-L6-3

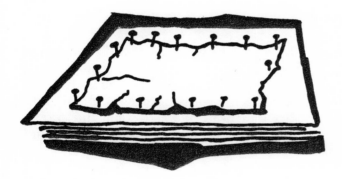

Figure 2-L6-4

newspapers, letting it completely dry to a crackle finish (Figure 2-L6-4).

7. Clean up by washing out brushes, storing the designs to dry in a safe location and collecting materials. Pour excess water down the sink and wash up.

Variations:

1. Use only brown ink or watercolors to create a leather-like surface. This can be used for book covers, portfolios or as a background for a crayon drawing.

2. Instead of using pins in the drying stage, use an electric iron to dry out the wet paper. The final effect will be less crackled, but much time can be saved.

Sliding the Paint Over!

Objectives:

1. To learn that wax crayons resist water soluble paints.
2. To learn to create a water color wash.

Materials:

Watercolor boxes, water cups, large watercolor brushes, crayons, 12 × 18-inch watercolor paper, newspapers.

Guidelines:

You've already learned that one of the most useful characteristics of wax crayons is the ability to resist water-soluble liquids. This characteristic of crayons has been advantageous in batiking and crayon resist techniques but it can also be useful for producing colorful backgrounds for your drawings. Combinations of water color and crayon result in an interesting technique that is easily completed in a brief hour's time.

Hold off thinking about the painting part of the activity and concentrate upon drawing ideas. Why not draw the interior of a large city store, or a milking barn in the country, whichever is most familiar to you? Sketch the large glass-covered counters in the store lightly with a brown crayon, add a few customers, the merchandise, a saleslady and you're ready for a sale. Don't forget the escalators and little old ladies with their shopping bags. In the barn, sketch in bundles of hay and a pitchfork, and a lantern or two. These details make a wonderful background and help to create the busy atmosphere within a large city store or the feeling of the barn.

Look over your crayon drawing, add a few more small details, such as pocketbooks, fur collars and cash registers and you're ready to mix the water color washes to spread over the crayon drawing. Use a large brush and a long stroke to cover those large paper areas. Start your washes at the top of each area and carry the wet paint down. This

64

will help you to create an evenly-colored wash and to cover the entire background of the crayon drawing in just a few minutes.

How to Do It:

1. Cover desks with newspapers and distribute watercolor boxes, water cups, brushes, crayons, paper and water to each pupil.

2. Use crayons to draw an interior scene on a piece of 12 × 18-inch watercolor paper (Figure 2-L7-1).

3. Mix large quantities of watercolors by dropping color into water in the beds at the top of the watercolor box (Figure 2-L7-2).

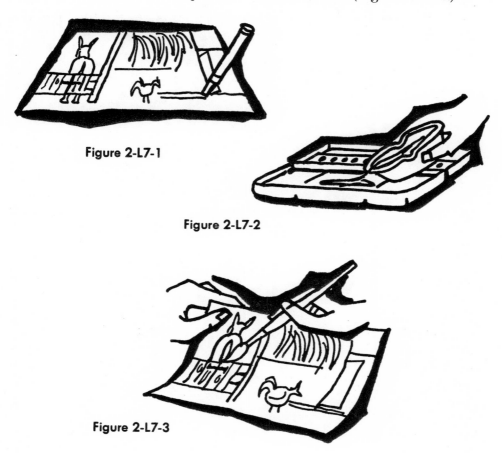

Figure 2-L7-1

Figure 2-L7-2

Figure 2-L7-3

4. Dip a large watercolor brush into the mixed color and paint entirely across the area being painted. Tilt the paper so that the edge

of the paint flows down the paper. Add more color with the brush until each area is completely covered with the proper color. Always keep the paper tilted while creating a watercolor wash (Figure 2-L7-3).

5. Clean up by folding newspapers and storing them away. Use Kleenex to clean and polish the watercolor boxes. Empty water cups into the sink and rinse them out. Place water cups to drain and wipe them dry later to prevent rusting. Wash up.

Variations:

1. Begin with the watercolor first. Paint in areas and add crayons over the painted surface.

2. Carry out the whole activity on paper plates and use them as a decoration.

CHAPTER 3

Painting with Variety and Style

INTRODUCTION TO PAINTING

Most children learn to paint in school rather than at home. Because of this, every classroom teacher needs to become aware of several basic factors important to learning about painting: (1) some paints, such as liquid or powdered tempera paint, are easier to use than others; (2) brush sizes are important to painting, since large background areas are difficult to paint using a small, pointed brush and details are impossible to paint using large brushes; and (3) there are specific types of painting paper to use with various kinds of paint. Painting on regular drawing manila paper is almost impossible.

Painting, along with learning to draw, is probably the most basic art activity that any pupil will experience. Painting is a functional part of many other types of art activities and, as such, deserves more classroom time than the majority of art guides call for. Painting skills develop slowly. Until elementary school pupils learn these skills, they are less likely to learn to paint spontaneously or creatively.

Painting Materials

The average elementary school classroom needs only three different types of brushes to complete most painting activities. These are: (1) a large watercolor brush, either size 12 or 13; (2) a small, pointed watercolor brush, ranging from size 6 to size 8; (3) a long-handled easel brush about 1/2 to 5/8 inches wide.

There are several types of water soluble paints that are practical in a classroom situation. For beginning painters, a powdered tempera paint mixed with water is most useful, although liquid tempera paint, thinned considerably, is the equivalent. Tempera paint usually requires some stirring and thinning if the paint has not been opened previously.

Watercolor paints are not usually introduced until second or third grade level in elementary schools since control of the free flowing paint is difficult and frustrating. Some classroom teachers find it useful to add a few drops of gloss starch to the water during the first few watercolor painting attempts. This additive hinders the flow of color somewhat, allowing the learner more time to control the paint.

Both tempera and watercolor paints may be combined with other art media to produce more variety and combinations for experienced pupils. This variety of mixed media can be extended even further if different types of painting surfaces are used. Each different painting surface will react individually to each kind of paint. Be sure to test paints and surface materials before each new activity.

Organizing for Painting Activities

Most painting activities generally follow similar organizational sequences: (1) motivation of a subject or theme; (2) demonstrations of new materials or techniques; (3) distribution of materials and tools; (4) the painting activity; and (5) cleanup and storage of materials. All, or any, of these steps can vary whenever it seems practical. In painting activities where materials must be shared by pupils, desks may be moved together to create a larger working surface. This is particularly useful whenever several different types of paint, or numerous materials, are used in one activity. Pupils may share a greater variety of materials and have a larger selection or choice in this organization.

Common Problems in a Painting

Frequently, pupils find themselves unable to add color to a painting or paint details in a picture. This occurs most often when pencils are used to sketch in the subject before painting. Pupils should be taught to sketch with a small watercolor brush, outlining their subjects by using the brush and a mixture of light brown color. The result is a sufficiently large drawing that can be painted easily.

Sometimes, color in a painting appears muddy or lacks intensity. When this occurs, observe the pupil at work, noting whether he cleans his brush between using different colors. When colors appear to be lacking in brightness and "washed out," encourage the pupil to use more color on his brush.

Some painters have difficulty drawing details with a brush. Instruct these pupils in the proper holding of a paint brush with the tip handle of the brush pointing high at the ceiling and fingers touching the metal ferrule. Brushes used at a low angle do not provide a small point to draw with!

Use the right paper for painting! A proper grade of painting paper will not absorb paint quickly. Most painting papers contain a sizing specifically for painting and are marked "Painting Manila" or "Watercolor Paper." Any paper that does not have one of these marks should be tested before you use it.

PAINTING

PAINTING ACTIVITY (GRADE LEVEL)	NEW MATERIALS INTRODUCED	PHYSICAL SKILLS INVOLVED	PUPILS LEARN	EMOTIONAL AND INTELLECTUAL EXPERIENCES
Painting Hand People (Watercolor hand puppets) (4-6)	Felt-Tip Watercolor Markers	Painting on flesh.	To create imaginary subjects.	Imagining Deciding Selecting
Sponge on Something (Tempera with sponges) (2-6)	Cello-Sponges	Applying paint with sponges.	To use different painting tools. To paint spontaneously and quickly.	Experimenting Trying Out Discovering
Pulling the String (Strings dipped in paint) (2-6)	String Folded Paper	Dipping string into paint. Pulling string ends.	To apply imagination to the non-objective. To add details to a painting.	Elaboration Deciding Selecting
Marble Paint (Floating paint on water) (5-6)	Oil Paint Paint Thinner	Dipping paper into a wet surface and removing it.	To create designs. That paint floats. That paint mixes.	Experimenting Trying out
Creating Transparently (Tissue and Paint) (2-6)	Colored Tissue Paper Liquid Starch Tempera Paint	Adhering colored tissue paper using starch. Painting in line with large brushes.	To create in line over colored backgrounds. To overlap colors. That two mixed colors create a third color.	Trying out Arranging Composing
Spraying Color (Spraying around Color Shapes) (5-6)	Spray Paint Cans Corrugated Cardboard Oak tag Drop Cloths	Cutting heavy cardboard. Spraying around stencils.	To create in a group situation. To work with large surface areas. To create stencils.	Experimenting Visualizing Composing
Flowers Like Water (Painting Wet) (3-6)	Watercolors Sponges Tempera paint Kleenex	Painting on a wet surface.	That flowing watercolor can be controlled. That wet paper surfaces require different painting techniques.	Composing Experimenting Visualizing
Transparent and Opaque (Powder Paint and watercolor) (5-6)	White Powder Paint Colored Background Paper	Painting solid silhouette shapes. Using watercolor in gouache technique.	To work with mixed media. To add color to basic shapes. To "tint" with color.	Selecting Visualizing Comparing Elaborating

Painting Hand People

Objectives:

1. To learn to paint designs using different materials and ideas.

2. To learn to combine art in a multi-disciplinary approach with language arts.

Materials:

Non-toxic, washable, felt-tip pens or Magic Markers, 12 × 18-inch white painting paper (optional), scissors, newspapers, paste, Kleenex tissues, newsprint, scrap colored paper, tissue paper.

Guidelines:

Have you talked to any puppets recently? You'll be surprised at how intelligent they are and how much these little people seem to understand everything you say! You can create several different kinds of puppets right on your hands if you have the right felt-tipped pens. If you are afraid of getting your own hands dirty, you can trace around your hand on paper and create a "substitute" hand. But it's more fun to paint directly on your own hand and watch your puppet grow into a real person.

Take a close look at the Magic Markers or felt-tipped pens that you use. They should be clearly marked non-toxic and water-soluble. Avoid those brands that are indelible or lack some consumer seal of approval.

Spread your fingers apart and use a pencil to outline around your hand on a piece of newsprint paper. Use this outline of your hand as an idea incubator to doodle with. Make as many outlines as you need. What shall your puppet be? A funny four-legged animal? A pink lady with three legs, or a funny old man with a mustache and beard? Use your own imagination to create whatever your doodling makes you think of.

After you've experimented with designing one or two puppets on paper you'll want to test your newly found art on its real surface

—your own hand! There are several different ways of doing this: (1) You may paint on the back of your hand, using either your wrist or fingers as the top of the head (see Figures 3-L1-2 and 3); (2) You may paint on the palm of your hand, or (3) You may clench your hand into a fist and paint (Figure 3-L1-4).

Use bright colors that contrast well against your skin. Add bits of tissues or other scrap materials that you may need to create your own humorous character. Remember, you're the person your puppet is going to talk to and complain about if you haven't done a good job!

How to Do It:

1. Move several desks together so that pupils may share different scrap materials and colors. Cover the desks with newspapers and distribute all papers, scrap materials, paste, scissors, felt-tipped pens and tissues to each group of pupils.

2. Use a pencil or marker to sketch around your hand on a piece of newsprint or scrap paper. Use felt-tipped pens to doodle on the drawn outline and think about ideas. Retrace around your hand on white paper and complete a puppet using felt-tipped pens if not painting directly on hands (Figure 3-L1-1).

3. When painting on your own hands use felt-tipped pens to draw your ideas directly on the skin. Either the back of the hand or the palm may be used in several different positions (Figures 3-L1-2 and 3). Hands may be clenched into a fist, or the palm of the hand with upraised fingers may be used as other positions (Figures 3-L1-4 and 5).

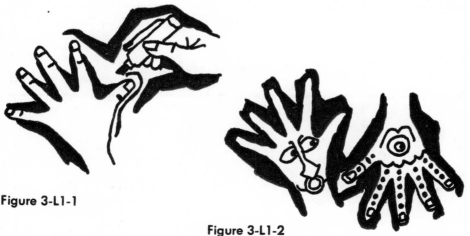

Figure 3-L1-1

Figure 3-L1-2

Figure 3-L1-3

Figure 3-L1-5

Figure 3-L1-4

4. Add small details to the painted puppet, using paste, colored paper, tissue paper, or any scraps that seem to fit the character of the puppet.

5. Clean up by replacing caps on felt-tipped pens, collect paste, scissors, and papers in scrap box. Throw away Kleenex tissues and small scraps. Wash up.

6. Use the puppets to write an original play.

Variations:

1. Make finger puppets for a quick activity, using the puppets in your reading group or social studies activity.

LESSON 2

Sponge On Something

Objectives:

1. To learn to paint spontaneously without pre-sketching ideas.

2. To learn to use a variety of painting materials.

Materials:

Cut up cellulose sponges, tempera paint, aluminum pie pans, 12

× 18-inch brush manila or white painting paper, one single-edge razor blade, watercolor cups, scissors, newspapers, Kleenex tissues.

Guidelines:

Here's one activity that won't require a lot of sketching and preparation before adding color to your painting. Using small pieces of sponges dipped in paint will enable you to paint directly and spontaneously right on the paper without drawing first.

Want to paint a tree? Just dip your sponge in the right color and start painting! Use your small pieces of sponge to build up several different colors for the foliage of a tree. Did you notice that the colors picked up by the sponge seem to blend into several different colors? Try using the side of the sponge to create those thinner lines you need in your painting, or cut a sponge into an even smaller piece using a pair of scissors. Watch out for dirty hands! You will find it difficult to keep your hands completely clean in this activity. Try to avoid touching your clothing and the drawing paper with your hands. Use a clean piece of Kleenex occasionally to wipe the paint from your hands. This will help to keep everything quite a bit cleaner!

Although the pieces of sponges you use to paint with can be almost any size or shape, the average size should be approximately an inch and one-half square. No need to measure! Use a single-edge razor blade to cut through large sponges. Large sharp scissors also may be used to cut even smaller pieces of sponge. Cut up several different sizes of sponge. Who knows what size you will need?

If you haven't tried sponge painting previously, try painting a landscape, seascape, or city scene. These subjects are familiar and include large objects and areas that are easier to paint with sponges. Avoid painting small objects and human figures until you have more experience painting with sponges.

How to Do It:

1. Pre-cut cellulose sponges using a single-edge razor blade or a pair of large scissors. Thin several colors of tempera paint to the consistency of thin cream (Figure 3-L2-1).

2. Move several desks together to facilitate sharing materials. Cover the desks with newspapers and distribute tempera paint in aluminum pie pans, or water cups, to each group of pupils. Three basic tempera colors and white are necessary for each group of four or five pupils. Distribute two pieces of sponge, a piece of painting paper and

Figure 3-L2-1

Kleenex to each individual pupil. Each group of pupils may share scissors used to cut sponges smaller whenever necessary.

3. Dip a piece of sponge into thinned tempera paint. Test the paint-loaded sponge on scrap newspaper before painting (Figure 3-L2-2).

4. Use the sponge to paint directly on paper (Figure 3-L2-3).

5. Use the edge of the sponge to paint any smaller lines that are needed in the painting (Figure 3-L2-4).

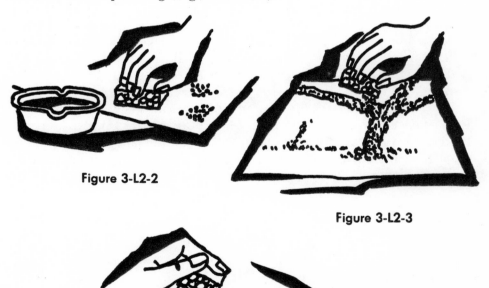

Figure 3-L2-2

Figure 3-L2-3

Figure 3-L2-4

6. Clean up by soaking sponges in a pail of water and squeezing these out later. Throw away scrap newspapers and run water over the aluminum pie pans or watercolor cups. Dry these with a towel to avoid rusting. Throw away excess used tempera paint. Collect scissors and wash up.

Variations:

1. Follow up the sponge painting activity by planning a small mural involving the complete class. No need to trim cellulose sponges for this larger activity.

LESSON 3

Pulling the String

Objectives:

1. To learn to use imagination in creating real subjects from non-objective shapes.

2. To learn to use a variety of painting materials.

Materials:

Lengths of soft cord or thick string, scissors, watercolor cups, 12 × 18-inch white paper, small watercolor brushes (size 7 or 8), toothpicks, newspapers, Kleenex tissues.

Guidelines:

It pays to exercise your imagination every now and then to prevent your brain from rusting. Here is one painting activity in which you can apply your best thinking and open up some new ideas.

There is no possible way to pre-determine what subject you are going to paint when you use string pulling as the basis of an idea. Who knows what you may see in the swirl of colors that evolve differently each time you pull the string through folded paper. Everyone sees different things, depending upon his experience and imagination.

Here's your chance to open up and think differently because no one else knows exactly what you know. Perhaps they don't see the lobster claw and body in that reddish blob because they've never been to Maine. Applying the same principle, perhaps you won't understand why your friend sees a roller coaster in that non-objective glob of colors that looks like nothing. That's what individualization is all about!

Be careful when you dip your string into a water cup half-filled with tempera paint. Perhaps it's better to use a toothpick to push the string under the paint surface rather than using your finger. Too much paint on the string? Not if you've thinned down the tempera paint and let the excess paint drip off the end of the string. Too much paint creates a blurry shape on the paper.

Don't think about where to place your string on the piece of folded paper, just let it fall where it may! Use two paint colors, any two, but select the lightest color of the two to use first. Light colors are not as visible over darker colors. Let a piece of string hang over the edge of the folded paper. You'll need a "handle" to pull with one hand as you hold down the folded paper with your other hand.

How to Do It:

1. Pre-cut two lengths of heavy string, or soft cord, into 24 to 36-inch lengths (Figure 3-L3-1). Thin some bright colors of tempera paint so that it flows freely (Figure 3-L3-2).

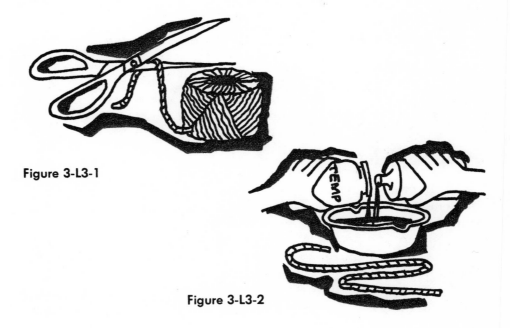

Figure 3-L3-1

Figure 3-L3-2

2. Move several desks together to create a larger working surface for pupils. Cover the desk area with newspapers to protect the surface. Distribute two watercolor pans half-filled with two contrasting colors of tempera paint, two pieces of string for each pupil, toothpicks or wooden matches, Kleenex tissues, small watercolor brushes and white paper to each pupil.

3. Fold a piece of white painting paper in half to produce two working surfaces 9 × 12 inches.

4. Dip most of the length of the string into the lightest color tempera paint. Use a toothpick, or wooden match, to push the string underneath the surface of the paint.

5. Remove the string filled with paint from the watercolor cup. Allow any excess paint to flow from the end of the string. Let the string fall freely on *one side* of the folded paper. A length of string should extend from the end of the folded paper (Figure 3-L3-3).

6. Fold the paper in half over the string. Use one hand to press down on the surface and the other hand to pull the end of the string out from between the folded paper (Figure 3-L3-4).

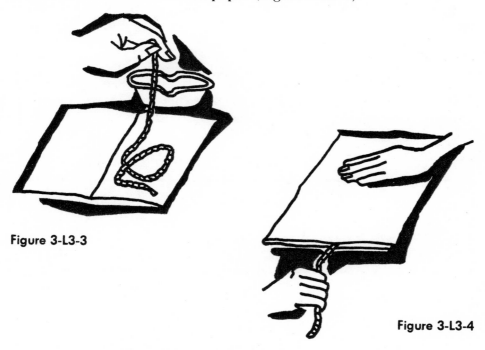

Figure 3-L3-3

Figure 3-L3-4

7. Repeat this same process using a second piece of string and a darker-color tempera paint.

8. Open the folded paper and observe the non-objective design that has resulted. Turn the design upside down and think about what real subject the colors and shapes remind you of.

9. Use a small watercolor brush to add any "extra" touches that will make your design more realistic (Figure 3-L3-5).

Figure 3-L3-5

10. Clean up by washing out brushes and laying them upon newspaper to dry. Throw away the string, used Kleenex tissues and soiled newspapers. Wash out watercolor cups and dry these to prevent rust. Wash up.

Variations:

1. For beginning activities, or with primary grades use one color instead of two. Discuss the subjects that various students see in their non-objective shapes.

LESSON 4

Marble Paint

Objectives:

1. To learn different techniques of painting.

2. To learn how to use the characteristics of different types of paint.

Materials:

A large white enamel or aluminum pan (minimum size 13 × 19 inches), water, several small (1/2 pint) cans of oil paint colors, odorless turpentine, tongue depressors, 12 × 18-inch white painting paper, empty cans to mix paint in, a scrap cloth towel, paper towels, news-paper for a drying area, Kleenex tissues.

Guidelines:

Marbelizing paper is one of the few ancient European arts still in existence that doesn't require time, patience and great skill. The secret of marbelizing is that thinned oil colors will float upon the sur-face of water; and when swirled with a spoon, will create many intricate designs that cannot be imitated.

You will find many opportunities to create quite a few mar-belized designs since it takes but a few seconds to place oil color on water, swirl with a wooden tool and place paper over the design. Re-moving the marbelizing paper from the pan and placing it on a pre-pared drying area takes only a few seconds more. The colors you use may be tubes of oil paint or, better yet, the small cans of oil mixing colors that paint stores use. Whichever color is used must be thinned with turpentine until it floats upon the surface of water. Test the thinned color by placing it gently on water. Some of the color will sink but some will also float. Every now and then clean the water surface in the pan by running a piece of highly absorbent paper towel across it. This activity helps to absorb the extra paint and clean the surface for future painting.

Test the paper you are going to use. Some, such as manila drawing paper, are too absorbent to use successfully. White painting-grade paper is usually always successful but testing your paper is rec-ommended. The oil colors seem to float well, although some colors of red spread too quickly to work with.

Since only one person at a time can marbelize a design in a pan, you must organize the work individually. Once your design has been completed you may think about what to use it for. Outside of the usual covers for programs, books and just plain painting designs, you may be able to think of different uses for marbelized paper. Use your creativ-ity!

How to Do It:

1. Place a pad of newspapers across the surface of a library table or large desk and some more on the floor as a drying area. Fill a large enameled pan with clean water (Figure 3-L4-1).

2. Use tongue depressors to thin oil paints with odorless turpentine (or paint thinner) in cans. Place these cans nearby the filled enameled tray (Figure 3-L4-2).

Figure 3-L4-1

Figure 3-L4-2

3. Distribute white paper to the pupils and have them write their names on the back of the paper. Organize the class so that two or three pupils are at the painting table at one time.

4. Have each pupil use the tongue depressors to place two oil colors gently on the surfaces of the water in the enameled pan. Use the tongue depressors to swirl the two colors together (Figure 3-L4-3).

5. Quickly place a piece of white paper over the design and remove the paper from the surface quickly. Bring the completed design to a drying area (Figure 3-L4-4).

6. Clean up by pouring water from the enameled pan into an old pail and pour it away outside in the earth. Use old towels and turpentine to clean out the enameled tray. Throw away used tongue depressors, newspapers and paper towels. Wash up with soap and

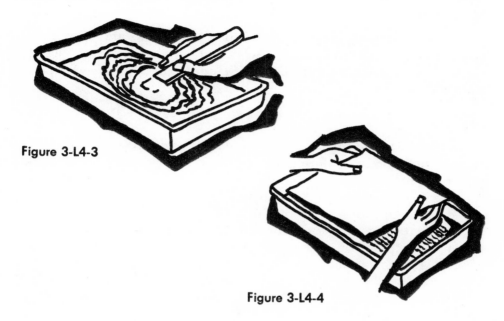

Figure 3-L4-3

Figure 3-L4-4

water after first using turpentine to clean oil paint from hands. Don't allow turpentine to remain on hands any length of time.

Variations:

1. Once the oil paint has completely dried, pupils can use the remaining paint to add *small* details to the marbelized backgrounds. Each background varies in color and design. Stimulate individual ideas by discussing what the different colors make you think about.

LESSON 5

Creating Transparently

Objectives:

1. To learn to use various combinations of painting materials.
2. To develop an understanding of color concepts.

Materials:

Colored tissue paper, 12 × 18-inch oak tag or lightweight cardboard, easel brush, gloss starch (without bluing), water cups, water, black tempera paint, a small (size 7 or 8) watercolor brush, newspapers, Kleenex tissues.

Guidelines:

Ready to see through it all and really begin to understand how color changes occur? Painting over transparent layers of colored tissue paper will help you to see what is happening and you will find that the "rules" of color hold true even though art media change.

Tear right into it! It's far better to tear lengths of colored tissue paper to create your colorful background, than it is to cut the tissue paper using a pair of scissors. Ragged edges of torn paper are more suggestive of forms in nature than clean-cut rectangular shapes. What bright colors will you use to create a seascape? Or do you want to select greens and browns to suggest earth colors? You'll need lots of scrap tissue paper to cover a 12 × 18-inch piece of oak tag background. You can use a paper background if oak tag or cardboard are not available, but the gloss starch you use to adhere the tissue paper tends to curl lighter background material quite a bit. Your final art work will require flattening out after it dries, if you use a lightweight material.

Thin gloss starch with a little water, just enough so that it flows more easily. Use a tough nylon bristle easel brush with gloss starch in lieu of a fine watercolor brush. Clean the starch out of your brush the same day you complete your painting. Don't permit starch to remain in a brush overnight.

Once the tissue paper background has been created, you are ready to start thinking about subjects that you want to paint over the background. Most of your ideas will probably relate to both the colors you've used in the background and the shapes of the torn tissue paper. What is it you see? Is that piece of brown tissue paper a clump of mesquite in Texas or a bush on Cape Cod, Massachusetts? Those long pieces of sand-colored tissue paper remind you of both places. Take your pick!

How to Do It:

1. Thin some gloss starch with water. Each pupil will need one water cup of starch. White glue, thinned with water, will prove an adequate substitute (Figure 3-L5-1).

Figure 3-L5-1

2. Move several desks together to create a larger working surface. Cover the desks with layers of newspapers and distribute cardboard, gloss starch in water cups, an easel brush and Kleenex tissues to each pupil. Retain the small brushes and tempera paint until pupils at each cluster of desks have completed the tissue background and are ready to paint.

3. Demonstrate applying glue to the cardboard background and how to apply tissue over the glue. Allow pupils from each table to select colored tissue paper from a central location.

4. Tear several strips of tissue paper into irregular shapes that completely cover the background (Figure 3-L5-2).

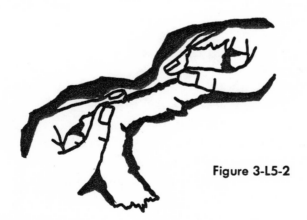

Figure 3-L5-2

5. Apply thinned gloss starch completely across part of the cardboard surface using an easel brush (Figure 3-L5-3).

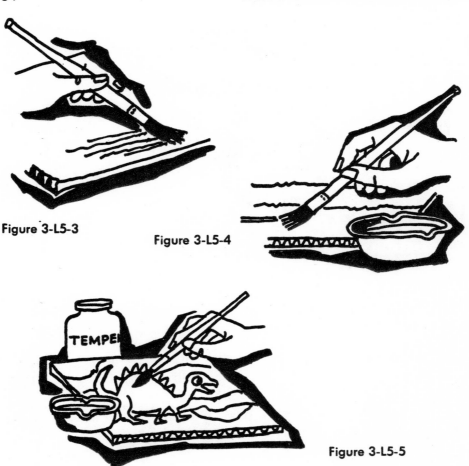

Figure 3-L5-3

Figure 3-L5-4

Figure 3-L5-5

6. Lay strips of colored tissue paper into the damp gloss starch, overlapping each color until the background is completely covered. Use the easel brush to smooth out most of the wrinkles that occur in the surface of the tissue paper (Figure 3-L5-4).

7. Add smaller pieces of torn tissue paper in an upright position over the background to "break up" the horizontal effect.

8. Once the tissue paper background has been completed use a small brush and black tempera paint to paint a scene or subject over it (Figure 3-L5-5).

9. Clean up by passing the scrap paper box to save large scraps of tissue paper. Collect the easel brushes and wash in soap and water as soon as possible. Wash out brushes and watercolor cups in water. Pass the waste paper basket for all scraps and dirty newspapers. Wash up!

Variations:

1. Embed small, flattened sticks or twigs under the colored tissue paper to create a landscape scene complete with people, trees and whatever else belongs in the picture.

LESSON 6

Spraying Color

Objectives:

1. To learn to paint using a variety of media and materials.
2. To learn to paint in group activities on large murals.

Materials:

16-ounce spray paint cans, large pieces of corrugated cardboard, 24 × 36-inch pieces of oak tag, pins, crayons, scissors, newspapers or a large painter's paper "drop" cloth, odorless turpentine, pieces of scrap cloth material.

Guidelines:

You won't "bomb" out in this art activity since you'll be using bombs in the form of cans of spray paint to create a large painting. Look around for some additional helpers because this activity will require lots of hands, especially if you are lucky enough to find an extra-large piece of corrugated cardboard.

Large pieces of corrugated cardboard are not difficult to locate. Try looking for mattress or refrigerator boxes at your local appliance dealers. These stores usually have boxes left over after uncrating their floor samples. Shop at the local paint or hardware store for several contrasting colors of spray paint to help make your mural distinct. Read directions on the spray can labels and follow these carefully. Spraying paint is very definitely an outside activity. After you have designed and cut your stencils from heavy oak tag inside, wait for a calm, breezeless day to complete your mural outside. Stick to one simple theme for your first spray mural and remember that the activity is really just a large stenciling technique. Flowers, trees, and dinosaurs, or other distinctly characteristic animals, are the easiest subjects for a large mural.

After everything is ready and stencils have been cut, prop the large cardboard background against a wall. Protect the ground and wall area from spray paint with a painter's large drop cloth. It's time to pin the stencils on the cardboard and test the spray paints. Remember! No wind. Spray paint can carry quite a distance in the air so select a lonely corner where a few drops of paint won't matter.

Wear your old clothes when you paint and stand close to the mural. A good distance to spray paint from is about two feet. Gather your helpers together to unpin the first layer of stencils and make ready for the next layer of spray paint. The more colors, the merrier!

How to Do It:

1. Select a subject for a stencil mural. Use crayons to draw subjects and details on large pieces of oak tag (Figure 3-L6-1).

2. Use sharp scissors to cut out the stencils (Figure 3-L6-2).

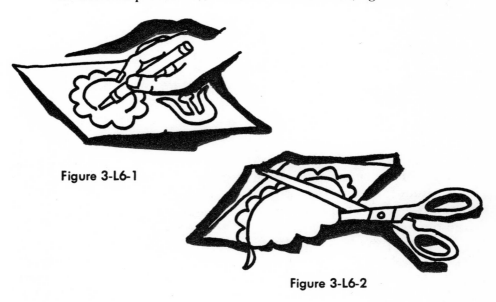

Figure 3-L6-1

Figure 3-L6-2

3. Use pins to stick the various stencils on a large corrugated cardboard background (Figure 3-L6-3).

4. Spread a painter's drop cloth under the corrugated card-

Figure 3-L6-3

board background to protect the ground and wall area from air-borne paint.

5. Stand back about two feet from the mural when spraying (Figure 3-L6-4).

Figure 3-L6-4

6. Remove the pinned stencils. Be careful to place these damp pieces of oak tag on newspapers to dry.

7. Pin new oak tag stencils for the second layer of color on the cardboard background and repeat the spraying process. Remove and repeat the process for each color that is used.

8. Clean up by throwing away used stencils. Dry and fold the drop cloth for further use. Store away crayons, scissors and large pieces of scrap oak tag. Use odorless turpentine and a cloth to remove paint from fingers. Always wash with soap and water after using turpentine. Lay turpentine-soaked cloths *outside* to dry.

Variations:

1. Create smaller stencils in the same manner with groups of two

pupils each, if large corrugated cardboard is not available. Limit beginning stencil mural efforts to two colors.

LESSON 7

Flowers Like Water

Objectives:

1. To learn to control watercolor paints on a damp paper surface.

2. To experience a spontaneous painting technique.

Materials:

Watercolor boxes, water cups, tempera paint, small and large watercolor brushes (sizes 8 and 12), large sponges, aluminum pie pans, 12 × 18-inch white paper of painting quality, newspapers, Kleenex tissues.

Guidelines:

One of the physical characteristics of transparent watercolor is its free-flowing quality. Add a damp paper surface to this specific characteristic and it will constitute quite a challenge for any painter. This is not an activity for beginning watercolorists so make certain that you have had some previous experiences with watercolor before attempting the more complex "wet-on-wet" painting technique.

Selection of the correct paper is very important to this painting activity. Manila drawing and white construction paper are too absorbent for use in the "wet-on-wet" painting process. A good quality white painting paper that will not absorb water quickly and allows the paper surface to remain damp long enough to paint upon is desirable. Test the paper you wish to use. If the paper remains fairly damp for a ten-minute period after the surface has been dampened, it is functional for this type of painting activity. Wetting the paper quickly is an important factor in the lesson. Since this is almost impossible with even large-size brushes, sponges are advisable.

You will need a large-size watercolor brush (size 12 or 13) that will hold more color. Large drops of watercolor, falling on damp paper, will form abstract, feathery-edged shapes that provide ideas to paint. Sometimes the paper becomes *too* wet and excess water collects in "pools" on the surface. Use dry Kleenex tissues to soak up some of this excess water without completely drying the surface.

Once your abstract shapes begin to dry, it is time to paint a subject over this colorful background. Use a smaller-size watercolor brush (size 7 or 8) and tempera paint to sketch your idea directly over the watercolor background. Tempera paint will not flow as freely on a damp surface as watercolor, so you need not worry about hurrying your painting. The combination of tempera and watercolor paints is a spontaneous one.

How to Do It:

1. Move desks together to create a larger working surface for small groups of pupils to share materials.

2. Use newspapers to cover the desks. Distribute large and small watercolor brushes, white painting paper and Kleenex tissues to each pupil. Prepare one or two water cups filled with black or purple tempera paint and distribute these colors with sponges and aluminum pie pans. Fill the pie pans with water (Figure 3-L7-1).

3. Dip the sponge into water and soak the paper surface. Remove any excess "pools" of water with a piece of dry tissue paper (Figure 3-L7-2).

Figure 3-L7-1

Figure 3-L7-2

4. Use a large watercolor brush "filled" with watercolor to drop color onto the wet paper surface. Repeat the process with other colors or the same color (Figure 3-L7-3).

5. After the surface has become fairly dry, use a small watercolor brush and tempera to paint a design or a realistic subject over the watercolor background (Figure 3-L7-4).

Figure 3-L7-3

Figure 3-L7-4

6. Add finishing details to the painting.

7. Clean up by washing out brushes and water cups in cold water. Use paper towels to dry the water cups and lay the damp brushes on dry newspaper. Use Kleenex tissues to wipe off any spots on the watercolor boxes. Squeeze out the sponges and throw away used Kleenex and newspapers. Wash up!

Variations:

1. Try the activity again after a period of time and notice the difference in the quality of ideas produced by pupils. Once pupils have gained security in using a familiar technique, they will begin to invent some variations of their own.

Transparent and Opaque

Objectives:

1. To learn to use a variety of paints and painting techniques.

2. To develop experience in composing and arranging elements within a painting.

Materials:

White, dry, powder paint, watercolor boxes, large and small watercolor brushes (sizes 12 and 8), water cups, water pitcher, 12 × 18-inch colored construction paper, newspapers, Kleenex tissues.

Guidelines:

Have you ever tried to paint a snow scene? It's not easy, especially if you're painting on manila or white painting paper. Whenever you get the feeling that you want to revel in a snow painting again, why not try using a piece of colored construction paper instead? That piece of cerulean blue paper that no one wanted to use all last year may be just the thing for a night skiing scene. Or that dull piece of maroon paper can be transformed into an ice skating scene complete with pond, people, and parks!

You must mix a dry, powdered tempera paint with water for the snow in this painting activity. Pre-mixed tempera paint will not function as well as powdered paint when used in combination with transparent watercolor. Better store a little extra water close to your painting, since dry tempera paint tends to thicken more quickly than most paints and will require some additional thinning with water as you move along in the activity.

Use a large watercolor brush, any size ranging from #11 to #14 will do, to *paint the entire winter picture in white*, as though in silhouette. This white is necessary to provide a background for the details, to be added by using watercolor paint. Watercolor is not visible when painted directly on colored construction paper, therefore the white paint acts as a "ground" for the transparent watercolor. It is probably wise to rinse out small watercolor brushes frequently in this painting activity. Painting onto white will cause the brush to pick up some paint, making it more difficult to keep the watercolors brilliant. Watercolor paint will "lay" on the surface of powdered tempera paint quite readily if not stroked back and forth too many times.

How to Do It:

1. Pre-mix dry white tempera powder with water to the consistency of very thin cream. Each pupil will need one water cup almost completely filled with this paint (Figure 3-L8-1).

Figure 3-L8-1

2. Move several desks together to create a larger working surface. Cover the surface of the desks with newspapers. Distribute a water cup of white paint, a large and small watercolor brush, Kleenex tissues, watercolor boxes and a water cup filled with water to each pupil. Allow pupils to select their own piece of construction paper from several different available colors.

3. Use a large watercolor brush and the mixed white paint to paint a winter scene in silhouette. Leave large areas of colored paper unpainted as a background (Figure 3-L8-2).

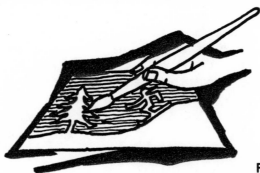

Figure 3-L8-2

4. Once the background painting has dried in some areas, use a small watercolor brush and watercolor paint to add color over the white paint. Try to avoid brushing watercolor paint in one area too long (Figure 3-L8-3).

5. Touch up areas that need more color or white paint (Figure 3-L8-4).

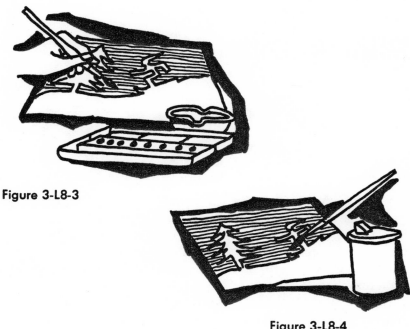

Figure 3-L8-3

Figure 3-L8-4

6. Clean up by washing out paint brushes and water cups. Dry the water cups and lay cleaned brushes on newspapers to dry. Use damp and dry Kleenex tissues to clean the watercolor boxes. Throw away scrap newspapers and wash up!

Variations:

1. Use a roll of colored construction paper, preferably blue or black, to create a mural using the same painting technique.

CHAPTER 4

Printing Different Things

INTRODUCTION TO PRINTING

Printing is always a successful art activity with young children because it involves physical activity and spontaneity, and does not require any high level of drawing ability. One need not be a great artist to create an original design and roll out ink over it. Most printing activities are fairly simple for elementary age pupils, requiring more patience than skill.

Most printing inks are water soluble, that is, they dissolve in water. These are the only type of printing inks recommended for elementary schools. There are many different ways of printing, ranging from a simple monoprint to the more complex linoleum block printing which requires knowledge of reversals and use of black and white as a form of "chiaroscuro," or three-dimensional effect. Monoprinting provides only one print; another design must be created if a second print is desired. Naturally, monoprinting is easier than multiprinting and is a natural art activity for both young and older elementary school pupils.

Printing Materials

In addition to water-soluble printing ink, you will need rubber roller-brayers to roll out the ink and a platen to roll the ink upon. Simple wire handle rollers are inexpensive and may be shared by pupils. There are many different platens that are functional in an elementary school, the simplest of which is a large vinyl floor tile. The non-absorbent characteristic of these floor tiles permits the ink to re-main moist longer. This is an important factor in printing.

The paper used to print upon should have the opposite quality of a printing platen; it should be absorbent. Most printing papers are clearly entitled so, but some papers may be used as substitutes with little loss in the quality of the final product. Soft paper finishes that are not polished or shiny may be used, such as newsprint, tissue paper or watercolor paper.

Materials used in printing activities can vary greatly. Almost anything, from macaroni and beans to gravestones, can be printed successfully. Various printing materials require slightly different approaches and modifications. All of these adjustments are clearly defined in each lesson found in this chapter.

Organization for Printing Activities

All printing lessons are group activities in which pupils share both tools and materials. Desks may be pushed together to create larger working surfaces. Surfaces should be covered with several layers of newspaper before materials are distributed.

Pupils should wear old shirts or smocks, whenever possible, to protect their clothes. Usually it is easier to print standing up as pupils tend to crowd closely around the table. There is the danger of wet printing ink rubbing off on clothes.

One of the most important parts of a printing activity is the establishment of an area for the wet prints to dry. One area of the classroom can be cleared and newspapers spread on the floor. Another method utilizes wire spread across one wall of the classroom, using bent paper clips to hang the wet prints on the stretched wire. Prints dry quickly on absorbent paper, but may not on a rainy day.

Cleanup takes longer in printing activities as most pupils get ink on their hands. Use a lot of soap and water and have a surplus of paper towels available for wiping up.

Common Problems in Printing Activities

Printing, like all art activities, poses some minor problems for pupils. On some days the printing ink tends to dry quickly. Keep a water cup available to add a few drops of water to the ink when it gets sticky.

Pupils who haven't printed before usually do not roll out the printing ink sufficiently. It takes more than a few moves over the ink-laden platen before inking the plate in a multi-print activity. The first print will require more ink and rolling than subsequent prints.

The most common barrier to good printing probably is using the wrong paper. There is no other way to determine whether ink and paper are compatible except to test them prior to the activity. If the print appears dry and weak after it has been prepared, try adding water to the ink or dampening the paper slightly. Either technique should improve the print.

Be certain you are using water-soluble ink. Read the labels carefully to ascertain that water is the diluting agent for the ink.

Cover up! Any pupils who tend to get dirty in other activities will certainly do so when involved in printing. Roll up sleeves, wear old shirts, have cleanup materials readily available.

PRINTING

PRINTING ACTIVITY (GRADE LEVEL)	NEW MATERIALS INTRODUCED	PHYSICAL SKILLS INVOLVED	PUPILS LEARN	EMOTIONAL AND INTELLECTUAL EXPERIENCES
Fold the Paper and Find The Idea (Folded paper and tempera) (K-3)		"Dropping" paint from a brush. Applying hand pressure to create a print.	To create a monoprint. To apply imagination to the non-objective.	Imagining Telling Visualizing
Printing What You Find (Prints of found Objects) (K-3)	Objects from Home Absorbent Paper Tempera Paint as a Printing Ink	Pressing to create an impression. Using proper amount of paint to paint.	That objects create prints. To overlap colors and printed lines. To select own materials.	Deciding Trying Out Seeing Selecting
Making Nature Work (Surface Rubbing) (K-6)	Objects from Home	Use a peeled-side crayon rubbed over textures.	That uneven surfaces can be printed by rubbing techniques. To overlap objects and create complex designs. To select their own materials.	Deciding Arranging Trying Out Selecting Touching
Rolling It Out (Brayer Rolling) (K-3)	Paper of Limited Size	Applying ink from a tube. Rolling a brayer in one direction.	That repetition of shapes creates design. To vary shapes and colors to create different designs. To plan a repetitive design in limited space.	Considering Comparing Experimenting Discovery
String Prints (String and Brayer) (4-6)	String	Rolling ink. Manipulating string.	That line creates design. To vary lines and create a variety of designs.	Arranging Evaluating Discovering
Corrugated Prints (4-6)	Corrugated Cardboard Scissors	Cutting heavy materials. Adhering materials. Rolling ink. Applying pressure to print.	That raised surfaces print. To use pressure to obtain a print. To create realistic prints.	Arranging Analyzing Visualizing
Spraying a Print (4-6)	Spray-Paint Cans Junk Hardware	Placing small pieces in an arrangement. Using a spray paint can for color.	To spray a monoprint. To create new spatial compositions.	Arranging Designing Composing
Digging into the Cardboard (Intaglio Printing) (5-6)	Flat Corrugated Cardboard Pencils as styli	Impressing line into a soft surface.	To create prints using only line drawing. That prints are reversals of drawings.	Arranging Composing Visualizing Touching

Fold the Paper and Find the Idea

Objectives:

1. To learn to create a monoprint.

2. To develop visual imagination and creative thinking about relationships between the "real" and the "abstract."

Materials:

12 × 18-inch manila paper, large watercolor brushes, small watercolor brushes, two water cups for each pupil, various colors of tempera paint, newspapers, water.

Guidelines:

A little paint, a piece of folded paper, a little pressure with the hand, and *voila!* you're well on your way to becoming involved with some of the most creative thinking possible. Here's an opportunity to use your imagination and practice a little originality. It's easy to be original in this printing activity because the thinking begins *after* you've created something. You're already halfway home; a little applied thinking completes the creativity.

Take a second look at the design you've created. Does it remind you of something you've seen before? Perhaps some animal you've seen pictures of, or a live lobster crawling across the bottom of the ocean. Add a few brush strokes for legs, eyes, and claws and watch your design turn into a lobster!

The sky is the limit! Let your imagination run wild. With a few, additional printed lines, your thinking will turn an unreal print into something real. Be sure to think of a fancy title for your foldover print, so that others will recognize what you've created.

How to Do It:

1. Organize the class into groups of three or four pupils. Push desks together to create a larger working surface. Cover the desk surfaces with sheets of newspapers.

2. Thin various colors of tempera paint with water so that the paint flows quite freely from a brush. Pour the prepared colors into paint cups and distribute two colors to each group of pupils. Use contrasting colors such as blue and orange, etc.

3. Supply a fairly large (size 12) and small (size 7 or 8) watercolor brush to each pupil. Each pupil should also receive a piece of 12 × 18-inch manila paper.

4. Fold the manila paper in half. The folded paper should be 9 × 12 inches (Figure 4-L1-1).

5. Open the folded paper. Dip a large watercolor brush into the prepared tempera paint. Remove the brush, allowing excess paint to drip from the brush into the fold and other areas of the manila paper (Figure 4-L1-2).

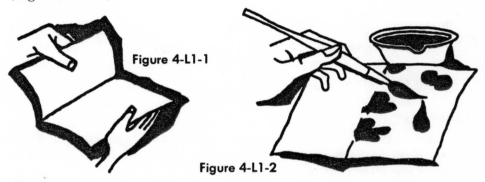

Figure 4-L1-1

Figure 4-L1-2

6. Repeat the process using another contrasting color of paint.

7. Refold the manila paper in half again. The paper surface facing you should be free of paint.

8. Press across the surface of the paper several times with the palm of your hand (Figure 4-L1-3).

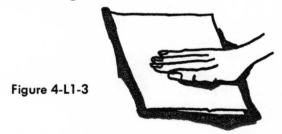

Figure 4-L1-3

9. Open the print. While it is drying ask "open-ended" questions about the design to motivate thinking. Offer contextual clues to those pupils who have difficulty visualizing a realistic subject.

10. Once a subject has been selected, encourage pupils to add details to the design that will help to make the subject more realistic (Figure 4-L1-4).

Figure 4-L1-4

11. Think of a title and write it in pencil, across the bottom of the painting. Add a signature.

12. Clean up by washing out brushes and paint cups and throwing away newspapers. Place the finished paintings on tables or the floor to dry.

Variations:

1. Use crayon, instead of paint, to add the realistic details. This will decrease the lesson time considerably.

2. Cut around the perimeter of each design using all the cutout designs to create one large bulletin board.

LESSON 2

Printing What You Find

Objectives:

1. To learn to create prints using common household objects.

2. To learn to overlap printed images, creating more depth in a print.

Materials:

Household objects; forks, funnels, potato mashers, sponges, egg slicers, etc.; scissors, aluminum pie tins, various colors of tempera paint, newspapers, newsprint paper, 18″ × 24″.

Guidelines:

Start looking around the kitchen and garage for small objects that have different, interesting shapes. You'll find lots of objects that can be used to print an unlimited variety of designs. These same objects can be used over and over again in many different combinations, so let variety be your goal.

Printing is simply reproducing images. You can use found objects to create your own original designs by dipping the object into a pan of tempera paint and pressing it onto paper. Sure it's simple: that's why object printing is so much fun. But also remember, your print can become as complicated as you want it to be.

Objects that have unusual contours are best for printing. Since the tempera paint must be washed off following the activity, use only objects that are easily cleaned. Poke around the kitchen for an old-fashioned potato masher; even that little bottle funnel can create two different size circles. Be certain that each object has a place where it can be held as you dip it into the paint.

How to Do It:

1. Organize the class into groups of three or four pupils.

2. Push several desks together to create a larger surface. Cover the desks or tables with newspapers.

3. Use other newspapers to cover a large section of the floor as a print drying area, or hang the wet prints on a cord stretched across the room using paper clips or clamps.

4. Mix several colors of tempera paint with water to a consistency of thick cream. Pour each color into individual pie tins, two colors for each group of four pupils (Figure 4-L2-1).

5. Distribute large sheets of newsprint to each pupil. Check to be certain that everyone has his object, paint and paper ready for printing.

6. Dip the object to be printed into the tempera paint. Remove the object from the paint, allowing any excess tempera to flow from the surface (Figure 4-L2-2).

Figure 4-L2-1

Figure 4-L2-2

7. Press the paint-covered object lightly on the surface of the newsprint (Figure 4-L2-3). Repeat this printing action on other areas of the paper.

Figure 4-L2-3

8. Use a contrasting color of tempera paint and a different object to overlap the first printed designs.

9. As each print is completed, sign your name and carry the print to the drying area. Prints will usually dry in 20 minutes under normal conditions.

10. Clean up by washing the household objects thoroughly with water, drying them with paper towels. Collect all newspapers in a basket. Pour any remaining tempera paint back into jars and wash out the aluminum pie tins. Look around for spots of tempera paint on the floor, desks and chairs.

Variations:

1. Have pupils trade objects using their new objects to create other prints.

2. Do not limit the prints to two colors, use several more colors in each print. This will result in a more colorful design.

LESSON 3

Make Nature Work

Objectives:

1. To learn to use side-crayon techniques.

2. To learn to select objects from nature as the subjects for art.

Materials:

Newspapers, dried pressed ferns, dried pressed flowers, small dried pressed plants or types of hay, soft wax crayons, tracing paper or tissue paper, manila paper, 12″ × 18″, white glue or paste.

Guidelines:

Save those ferns, strands of hay, and posies that bloom early in the spring. Even the pesty timothy that keeps cropping up in your backyard may be useful for this activity!

Collect a variety of different-sized small plants and flowers for this activity—classifying and naming them may be scientific fun too! You'll find pressing and drying plants can be an easy task. Forget the old-fashioned weighted-book method. Not only do flowers and plants stain the books, but the drying process takes too long. Make it easy on yourself and save time by placing all the plants you've collected between two large desk blotters. Use the heaviest objects you can find as weights over these two blotters. A piece of 1/4-inch plywood placed directly over the blotters will help to spread the weight evenly, accelerating the drying process. After a few days, the plants are usually pressed flat enough to use in the activity.

Arrange the plants on paper to your heart's content—you are the artist. Overlap some plants, shift other plants around on the paper. Experiment—your composition will be all the better for it.

Have patience, once you've glued down the dried plants. You'll have to wait a day before you can begin your crayon rubbing. So you really have two lessons for the price of one.

How to Do It:

1. Collect a variety of dried plants throughout the fall or spring. Press and dry these plants several weeks prior to the activity (see Guidelines). Each pupil should collect and press a minimum of 20 plants in preparation for the activity.

2. Distribute thick pads of newspaper to each pupil. (The equivalent of a full daily newspaper is sufficient.) Each pupil will also require a minimum of two sheets of tissue paper (or tracing paper) and a piece of 12 × 18-inch manila paper.

3. Distribute tubes of white glue to each pupil, or pour a small amount of white glue on a piece of scrap paper for each pupil to use.

4. Begin by arranging dried plants on the manila paper. Experiment with various compositions until satisfied. Use white glue to adhere these plants into the selected position. Allow time for drying (Figure 4-L3-1).

5. Peel all the paper from a soft wax crayon.

6. Place the completed arrangement of plants on a pad of newspapers. Cover this with a sheet of tissue paper (or tracing paper) and cut to a similar size. Use paper clips to fasten the two pieces of paper together (Figure 4-L3-2).

Figure 4-L3-1

Figure 4-L3-2

7. Lay a peeled crayon flat upon the tissue paper. Using pressure, pull, not push, the crayon across the surface of the tissue paper. The crayon must lay flat on the paper at all times as it is pulled across the paper surface. Repeat this process until the image of the dried plants becomes visible on the tissue paper (Figure 4-L3-3).

Figure 4-L3-3

8. Remove the rubbing and try another print.

9. Clean up by throwing away scrap papers. Stack salvageable newspapers in the closet for future use and wash up!

Variations:

1. Motivate pupils to draw small details on the print by telling stories about "imaginary" insects or animals who live in the plants.

2. Try shifting the tissue paper a few inches after completing the first print. Use a darker-colored crayon to create a second rubbing over the first.

LESSON 4

Rolling It Out

Objectives:

1. To learn to create repetitive designs through using a brayer.

2. To learn about the printing process and how to use the basic tools.

Materials:

Printing brayers, various colors of water-soluble printing ink, white paper strips pre-cut to 6 × 12 inches. Kleenex tissues, water, paint cups, newspapers.

Guidelines:

If you've never printed anything before, this is the way to start. This printing technique is simple enough for a four-year old and still exciting enough for anyone else. It must be the manipulative action of the printing brayers that keeps everyone interested. At least it keeps you busy!

Printing with a brayer is simple but it is also an excellent introduction to learning about repetition of shapes and colors, one of the basic elements of design that professional artists use. It is also basic to border designs used by both the American Indians and American craftsmen in the eighteenth century.

Brayer printing is a spontaneous activity, involving the learner immediately in squeezing and rolling out ink on paper. Since every step of the activity is so simple there is ample time to experiment with several different designs. You'll have lots of time to think of new designs or add lines to the old designs.

Many different kinds of paper are functional when printing with water-soluble inks. Any thin non-absorbent type of paper, such as tissue paper is usable. Absorbent papers, such as manila paper, tend to "soak up" the ink too quickly, so choose the "right" paper to print on.

How to Do It:

1. Organize the class into groups of 4 or 5 pupils.

2. Pre-cut several 6 × 12-inch strips of paper for each pupil.

3. Cover tables, or desks pushed together, with newspapers. Distribute several tubes of water-soluble ink to each group of 4 pupils. Each individual pupil will require a printing brayer and several strips of paper to print on.

4. Squeeze the ink directly from the tubes onto the surface of the brayer (Figure 4-L4-1).

5. Repeat this process using other colors.

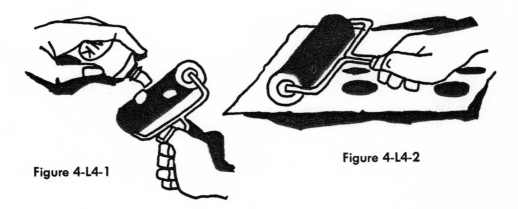

Figure 4-L4-1

Figure 4-L4-2

6. Roll the inked brayer completely over the paper in one complete stroke without hesitating (Figure 4-L4-2).

7. Print on other types of paper, varying the shapes and ink colors squeezed onto the brayers.

8. Clean up by washing brayers in the sink and rolling them dry on scrap newspapers. Throw away scrap pieces. Replace the tops on the tubes of ink and wash up.

Variations:

1. Squeeze one color of ink directly over another color on the brayer, creating a mixed color on the final print.

2. Cut the final prints into small pieces and glue all of these together on a large piece of cardboard to create a larger arrangement.

LESSON 5

String Prints

Objectives:

1. To learn to use various printing materials and techniques.

2. To learn to use a printing brayer skillfully.

Materials:

Roller brayers, various colors of water-soluble printing inks, a variety of printing papers, vinyl floor tiles, paper towels, water, paint cups, string, newspapers.

Guidelines:

With a little bit of experience using printing brayers, you're ready to conquer the more difficult technique of adding materials to the brayer. Although there are a great variety of materials you can successfully add to a brayer, string is perhaps the easiest to work with. One ball of string will provide enough material to make prints that will stretch around the schoolyard! Inexpensively too!

Because printing is a spontaneous activity, there's no way of predicting just how many prints anyone will be able to produce. Be ready with plenty of paper cut into 6 × 12-inch strips. Longer strips can be cut from standard size paper to help vary the sizes of your prints.

There are very few problems to solve when printing with string added to a brayer. Sometimes the string is not "picked up" by the brayer on the first attempt, but rolling back over it again usually cures this fault.

Don't worry about design! Brayer printing creates design automatically because it repeats colors and lines as the brayer rolls along, and this is what design is all about. Roll out designs to your heart's content!

How to Do It:

1. Organize pupils into groups of four or five.

2. Push desks together to create a larger surface area and cover with newspapers. Distribute brayers and pre-cut printing papers to each pupil. Distribute two vinyl floor tiles and two different colored tubes of printing ink to each group.

3. Fill water cups half way with water and distribute one to each group.

4. Squeeze about three inches of water-soluble ink from the tube onto a vinyl floor tile. Add a drop of water (Figure 4-L5-1).

5. Using a brayer, roll the ink out evenly on the tile until it is smooth and creamy (Figure 4-L5-2).

6. Cut off a 12 to 18-inch length from a ball of string. Place this

Figure 4-L5-1

Figure 4-L5-2

string on a flat surface covered with newspapers and roll the inked brayer over the string until it is "picked up" on the brayer (Figures 4-L5-3 and 4).

7. Roll the inked brayer over the pre-cut paper (Figure 4-L5-5).

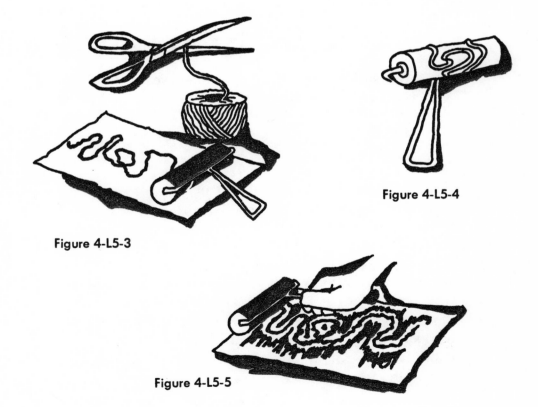

Figure 4-L5-4

Figure 4-L5-3

Figure 4-L5-5

8. Clean up by washing brayers in the sink and rolling dry on newspapers. Throw away scraps, replace tops on the ink tubes and wash up!

Variations:

1. Overprint some prints with other darker colors of ink, producing a two-color print.

2. Have pupils trade prints and print their own designs over other pupils' "extra" prints.

LESSON 6

Corrugated Prints

Objectives:

1. To learn to create "line" in printing.

2. To learn to create prints from raised surfaces.

Materials:

Printing brayers, corrugated cardboard, heavy cord or a flexible twine, white glue, vinyl floor tiles, tubes of black, water-soluble printing ink, newspapers, tissue or block-printing papers, black crayons, scissors, paper towels.

Guidelines:

Here's a printing activity to stimulate your imagination. That length of cord you cut from a ball can be the beginning of almost any subject—real or unreal! Cord can be twisted into any shape you desire, if you dampen it. As you're manipulating the cord and trying out different things, you'll discover many new ideas. Once you've decided on your final idea, a little glue will help to make it permanent and ready for the printing process.

Don't stop with just an outline of an octopus—let that string go to work for you and create other details. Perhaps your octopus needs eyes, other fish to swim with, anything you think of!

Don't worry about printing ink filling in the spaces between your designs; these black and white contrasts always add more depth to the final print. Create as many prints as you want, the plate will last for quite a while.

How to Do It:

1. Cut several pieces of tissue, or block-printing paper, for each pupil. Standard 12″ × 18″ size is large enough to design upon. Pre-cut corrugated cardboard to a size slightly smaller than the paper size.

2. Push desks together for each group of four pupils to share materials. Cover the desk thoroughly with newspapers.

3. Locate a drying area nearby and cover this area with newspapers also.

4. Pre-cut cord to various lengths ranging from 3 feet to 4 feet. Distribute all the materials required for the activity. Pupils may share the vinyl floor tiles and printing inks.

5. Use the black crayon to draw a design on the surface of the corrugated cardboard (Figure 4-L6-1).

Figure 4-L6-1

6. Dampen the cord under water in the sink to make it more flexible. Use a paper towel to squeeze out any excess water.

7. Using white glue, adhere the string to the design on the cardboard. Follow the drawn crayon line carefully. Add other details with smaller pieces of cord. Allow time for the string to dry (Figure 4-L6-2).

Figure 4-L6-2

8. Roll out black, water-soluble printing ink on a vinyl floor tile. "Work" the ink until it rolls out smoothly and easily on the tile surface.

9. Roll the inked brayer over the string surface until the string is completely covered with ink. This will take a few extra minutes for the first print (Figure 4-L6-3).

10. Place a piece of printing paper over the inked surface. Use a large wooden spoon (preferred), or the palm of your hand, to press the paper onto the inked cardboard plate. Make sure your hands are clean (Figure 4-L6-4).

Figure 4-L6-3

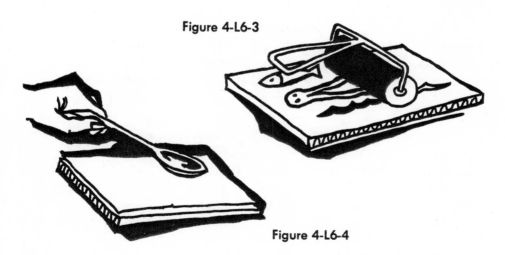

Figure 4-L6-4

11. Pull the print off and place it in a safe location to dry.

12. Wash the vinyl floor tiles and brayers under water in the sink. Look for ink "spots" on chairs and desks. Throw away scrap newspapers and unusable materials.

Variations:

1. Use two colors of ink on the same design.

2. Let string fall randomly on a cardboard surface and then glue the string to the cardboard surface. Add details to the print with pieces of oak tag combined with the cord.

LESSON 7

Spraying a Print

Objectives:

1. To learn about contrasting spaces in designs.
2. To learn to use household objects in creating art.

Materials:

Several deep corrugated boxes, additional pieces of corrugated cardboard, cans of black spray paint, sheets of white cardboard or heavy white paper to print on, an assortment of old nails, screws, and other used hardware, paint thinner, cleanup rags, newspapers.

Guidelines:

Wondering what to do with the collection of junk, small odds and ends, and old hardware that accumulated just in time for the annual spring cleaning? Rest assured that these metal scraps will be put to good use in the creation of a monoprint. It's so simple a process that even young beginners are highly successful.

Why not share the fun with a partner? Working together will help produce more ideas and variety.

Thinking about designs, composing, or what theme to develop? Forget all about it! This is *truly* an experimental activity within the easy reach of everyone. Just pick up a handful of your scrap hardware pieces and let them fall where they may on a piece of white cardboard. Spraying paint around this random composition produces a contrasting, finely-detailed print. But better be certain that the print is at the bottom of a large cardboard box at least 15 inches deep, or the paint will fly into unwanted areas. Better handle the wet prints by yourself, no sense in two people getting paint on their hands.

It's permissible to change the position of any objects you want to, but this is seldom necessary since Luck appears to be a pretty good designer "herself."

How to Do It:

1. Place several large boxes in corners of the room. These boxes should be at least 15 inches deep and spacious enough to fit a 12 by 18-inch piece of cardboard on the bottom surface. Tape papers on the wall behind the boxes and spread other newspapers underneath them to protect surfaces from spray paint.

2. Distribute all materials required for the activity. Pupils will share spray-paint cans and boxes at the printing areas.

3. Place a piece of white cardboard, or paper, on a slightly larger piece of corrugated cardboard that has been pre-cut to size. This cardboard is used to carry the arrangement to the spraying area.

4. Scatter small pieces of hardware at random across the paper surface (Figure 4-L7-1).

5. Make any changes in the composition as desired.

6. Place the completed arrangement on the cardboard base at the bottom of a box (Figure 4-L7-2).

7. Using a spray can of black paint, spray evenly over the hard-

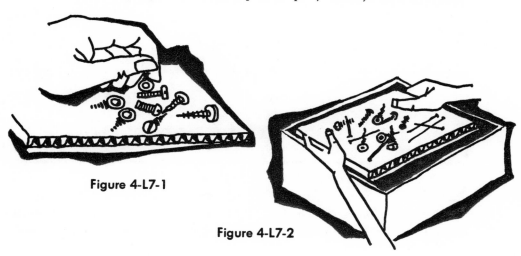

Figure 4-L7-1

Figure 4-L7-2

Figure 4-L7-3

ware. *Do not* spray too long, a light coat is sufficient. Keep windows in the room open for cross ventilation (Figure 4-L7-3).

8. Have one person hand!e and remove all the wet prints, placing these on newspapers to dry.

9. Clean up any paint spots with rags dipped in paint thinner, avoid using turpentine. Any paint on hands can be cleaned with paint thinner. Always end up washing hands with soap and water. Throw away the waste materials and store the spray paint for future activities. Follow the directions on the spray can for cleaning the nozzle for future use.

Variations:

1. Overlap all the prints on a large bulletin board, creating a lively display of contrasting designs.

2. Substitute a flexible cord, or twine, for the hardware and repeat the activity for an easier lesson.

3. Add bright light spots of color to the design with brush and acrylic paint or other spray paints.

LESSON 8

Digging into the Cardboard

Objectives:

1. To learn to create a simple print from non-raised surfaces (intaglio).

2. To learn the skill of printing fine lines.

Materials:

Corrugated cardboard, hard lead pencils, large wooden spoons, tubes of black, water-soluble printing ink, vinyl floor tiles, printing brayers, tissue paper or newsprint, newspapers.

Guidelines:

Gutenberg would have been proud of this type of printing, easily accomplished by anyone who can draw a line with a pencil. A "negative" print is produced; what is drawn is light, what is left alone is dark. This drawing can be used to produce several copies! Gutenberg better watch out!

Better keep the print small, it's easier to work on a small plate. Corrugated cardboard between 8 × 10 and 10 × 12 inches makes excellent size plates. Be quick about rolling out the ink, placing the printing paper, and pressing the print, because printing ink is quickly absorbed into the soft surface of cardboard. You'll probably work harder on the first few coats of printing ink than you will on succeeding coats, at least until some of the ink sinks into the surface and seals the cardboard.

Press hard on that hard lead pencil after you've first drawn your design, the deeper the line is drawn into the cardboard surface, the less likely it is to be filled in with ink. Be safe and go over the drawing twice. Use the inked brayer carefully, trying not to fill in the incised drawn lines.

How to Do It:

1. Create a printing plate by pre-cutting pieces of corrugated cardboard on a paper cutter to a maximum of 9 × 12 inches. Also pre-cut print paper to a slightly larger size.

2. Distribute all the required materials for the activity. Pupils may share tubes of ink, vinyl floor tiles and brayers, if necessary.

3. Select a hard lead pencil (number 2-1/2 or 3). Dull the lead point slightly by rubbing the pencil point on scrap paper. Sharp points tend to break more easily.

4. Use the pencil to draw a subject or design on the surface of the corrugated cardboard. Sketch the subject lightly without attempting to incise or dig into the cardboard surface at first (Figure 4-L8-1).

Figure 4-L8-1

5. Add more details to the drawing or design.

6. Retrace the drawn lines, pressing into the cardboard as deeply as possible.

7. Roll water soluble ink on the surface of a vinyl floor tile using a printing brayer. Continue rolling the ink until the ink is smooth.

8. Roll this ink evenly over the corrugated cardboard print. Avoid using heavy pressure on the brayer. Too much pressure on the brayer tends to fill in the incised lines with ink (Figure 4-L8-2).

9. Place a piece of printing paper (tissue paper, newsprint, or block-printing paper) over the inked design. Speed is desirable at this point of the activity (Figure 4-L8-3).

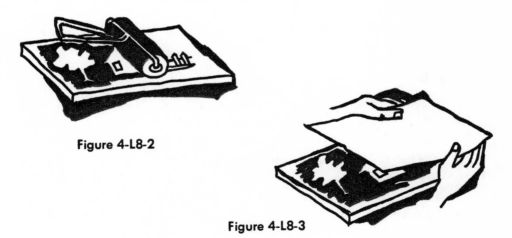

Figure 4-L8-2

Figure 4-L8-3

10. Use the palm of your hand, or a large wooden spoon to completely rub the surface of the print. Lift up one corner of the print

to check on the quality of the print. Repeat rubbing if sections of the print are not visible (Figure 4-L8-4).

Figure 4-L8-4

11. Pull the print from the plate and place it in a safe place to dry.

12. Wash the vinyl floor tiles and brayers under water in the sink. Throw away soiled newspapers and scrap materials. Wash up with soap and water.

Variations:

1. Print the same print twice, using two light-colored inks (yellow and orange). Shift the second print to one side about one inch to create a double image.

CHAPTER **5**

Creating with Paper

INTRODUCTION TO PAPER

Creating with paper is probably one of the most highly under-rated art activities in contemporary elementary school art programs. Pupils relate to manipulating paper easily, soon developing the various skills required to create both flat and three-dimensional art work.

Skills used in creating with paper can be developed gradually. At early ages, pupils learn to cut circles and squares, as well as small and large pieces of paper. As they gain experience in using paper, they advance to more complex skills and activities, such as tearing paper, curling, cutting through several layers of paper and learning to compose pictures entirely from colored paper. With all these experiences and skills behind them, older elementary school pupils are ready to create paper mosaics, learn to "score" flat paper to produce three-dimensional effects and to combine a great variety of paper materials, such as boxes, transparent papers and collage materials into original designs.

Although physical motor and manipulative skills are important to development and success in working with paper, there are emotional and intellectual experiences that should not be overlooked. Experimenting with paper involves pupils in: arranging and composing with different materials; exploring a variety of methods and techniques; trying out new and imaginative ideas; making decisions and judgements about visual problems; discovering the concepts of space and depth through overlapping objects and learning to compose spatially.

Now, tell the truth, did you *really* think your class was involved with so much thinking when they worked with paper? They certainly are!

Paper Materials

Elementary school pupils should explore a variety of paper materials and techniques in order to reinforce their skills using this medium. Pupils begin to learn about paper by tearing and cutting colored poster paper and construction paper. Skillful cutting is developed through many guided experiences and activities.

As pupils progress in their skills, they are able to create abstract designs and realistic pictures using transparent colored tissue paper, combine a variety of materials with paper and learn to use different types of paper such as oak tag, wax paper, saran wrap, colored cellophane and corrugated cardboard.

There is a natural progression from cutting flat paper to creating three-dimensionally with the same material. This development involves pupil growth, maturation and awareness. Concepts and techniques related to paper activities grow along with pupil experiences. Children do not learn about three-dimensional paper sculpture spontaneously; success is gradually developed from previous experiences. Some activities, such as "scoring" (folding and creasing) heavy white paper, are physically difficult for very young pupils; however, these same pupils can be introduced to three-dimensional paper through manipulating construction paper and colored oak tag. Elementary age pupils who have experienced working with a variety of paper activities are capable of creating with various combinations of materials and techniques. They can explore sculptural forms using boxes, corrugated cardboard and paper sculpture.

Organizing for Paper Activities

Most paper activities are aimed at the individual pupil to stimulate personal originality. Some activities, however, are best organized for small groups to take advantage of sharing materials such as white glue, varieties of colored paper, boxes, and small tools.

Desks and tables should always be protected by newspapers from glue, paste, and mars caused by scissors and stencil knives. Most pupils work fairly cleanly with paper and do not require smocks or old shirts to protect them from smears and spills.

A variety of small tools are vital to creating with paper. Hand staplers are useful to attach paper shapes together, although some models are too bulky for younger students to use. Try to find smaller-size, hand-held, staplers. Activities that require adults to assist at "crucial" points should be avoided. Art activities should make pupils feel successful and creative. This attitude cannot be fulfilled if teachers "help" too much.

Cleaning up after paper activities is fairly easy. There are a variety of materials to organize after a lesson. Scrap paper is valuable for many other art activities and large pieces should be collected diligently following each paper activity—every scrap piece saves budget funds for more expensive art materials.

Common Problems Using Paper

Some pupils are more capable of creating with paper than others are. There is only a casual relationship between pupils who are successful in drawing and painting and those who create successfully using paper.

Observe your class when they are involved in a paper activity. Look carefully for those pupils who work spontaneously and skillfully with the medium. Guide these pupils in future activities to higher-level activities.

Some pupils are not neat, especially when applying paste or glue. Although the repetition is sometimes boring, before each paper activity emphasize the rules of using glue and paste. Stress keeping *one* finger for applying paste. Provide paper towels for wiping purposes. Constantly stress cleanliness until it occurs.

Using white glue to adhere heavier objects, such as corrugated boxes, requires patience, as well as good directions to pupils. White glue does not "set" quickly and elementary age pupils are prone to handle their art products before the pieces are completely dried. Stress that moving three-dimensional sculpture should be avoided. It takes several hours for white glue to dry completely and pupils should be made aware of the consequences when the drying process is interrupted.

Pupils who do not use scissors correctly should be instructed how to hold the scissors and what part of the blade should be used for cutting.

Any new tools, such as stencil knives, should be demonstrated before the total class. Safety rules should be stressed consistently.

CREATING WITH PAPER

PAPER ACTIVITY (GRADE LEVEL)	NEW MATERIALS INTRODUCED	PHYSICAL SKILLS INVOLVED	PUPILS LEARN	EMOTIONAL AND INTELLECTUAL EXPERIENCES
Creating Bulletin Boards (5-6)	Pipe cleaners Staplers Large construction paper rolls	Cutting paper. Stapling shapes. Twisting pipe cleaners together. Pasting.	To create a three-dimensional mural. To overlap shapes and compose in large areas.	Arranging Composing Planning Judging
Shoebox Dioramas (3-6)	Boxes Materials from nature	Gluing various materials. Creating small details.	To overlap subjects. Creating depth. To arrange various materials.	Creating Depth Arranging Materials Deciding
Oaktag Masks (4-6)	Oak tag Staples	Pasting. Cutting. Curling paper. Manipulating materials.	To estimate and judge space. To create imaginatively. To elaborate small details.	Elaboration Evaluation Judging Imagining
Corrugated Box Animals (5-6)	Corrugated cardboard Small boxes	Gluing heavy objects. Cutting small details. Curling and scoring paper.	To construct dimensionally. To use their imagination. To plan ideas.	Imagining Constructing Elaborating
Weaving Paper (2-3)	Staplers	Freehand cutting. Manipulating paper.	The basic weaving process.	Touching Discovering
Circles and Squares (K-2)	Construction paper	Cutting specific shapes. Trimming with scissors. Pasting paper.	To create basic shapes. To paste cleanly. To modify.	Arranging Composing Synthesizing Visualizing
Scoring Paper (4-6)	Heavy white paper Stencil knives Large paper backgrounds	Scoring heavy paper using scissors. Cutting out shapes using stencil knives. Stapling shapes.	To create shapes and textures. To work in groups on a single theme.	Creating Visualizing Evaluating
Tearing Paper (3-6)	Various weights of paper Paper clips	Cutting through several layers of paper. Tearing paper. Pasting.	To compose backgrounds. To overlap shapes. To cut several similar shapes simultaneously.	Composing Visualizing Deciding Imagining
Saran Wrap (4-6)	Saran wrap	Cutting through several layers of paper. Overlapping pasted shapes. Rolling out adhesive paper.	To overlap shapes. To create backgrounds and add details. To plan complex pictures.	Planning Deciding Elaborating Imagining
Dyeing Paper (3-6)	Cold water dyes Absorbent paper Towels Large bowls	Dipping paper in dye. Folding paper in various shapes.	To create repetitive color patterns. To fold various paper shapes. To create multiple designs.	Creating Experimenting Planning Designing

Circles and Squares Make Anything!

Objectives:

1. To learn to cut various geometric shapes freehand.

2. To learn to create various subjects from simple basic shapes.

Materials:

Colored construction paper, scissors, school paste, paper towels, paper cutter, newspapers.

Guidelines:

A famous artist once said, "Anything that man or nature created can be imitated geometrically"—and cubism was born. This artist spoke truthfully; most objects can be visualized using squares, circles and rectangles. Observe very young children playing with wooden blocks to see how early in life this visual understanding begins. These youngsters apply their imagination to block building, creating lions, trucks, anything they think is important at the moment!

Cut now, create later! Don't worry about a subject right away —start cutting. The paper cutter comes in handy to prepare two-inch wide strips of various-colored construction paper. You will probably need two or three of these 12-inch-long strips for each design.

See how easy it is to cut a square or rectangle straight through the width of the strip. A circle? Easy! Just pick up one of the already cut squares and trim around the four corners. A bit more trimming and out pops a circle.

What shall we make out of all these geometric shapes? A tree? Simple—just place that rectangle together with a few circles at the top. A car? This time the rectangle goes on top and the circles underneath for wheels. It won't be cheating if you want to cut out a tiny circle or square for the headlights or windows—feel free to add small details to the basic form.

Experiment by trying to create different objects from the geometric shapes. Use black, or other dark-colored construction paper, as the base color for your design. Try to think of different subjects. Your thinking will begin to accelerate once the first circle is set in place. Be a neat paster! Use only one finger for pasting and keep the other fingers clean. Use a paper towel to wipe the paste from your fingers occasionally. Luckily, the desk was covered with newspapers! There, you're all finished! Better sign the masterpiece now.

How to Do It:

1. Use a paper cutter to cut two-inch strips from bright-colored, 12 × 18-inch construction paper. Each pupil will need two or three of these 2 × 18-inch strips and a dark-colored paper background (Figure 5-L1-1).

2. Cover the desks with newspapers. Distribute scissors, paste, the pre-cut strips, and a piece of 12 × 18-inch, black construction paper.

3. Cut across the short width of the colored paper strips to create two-inch squares. Use your visual judgement without measuring exactly (Figure 5-L1-2).

Figure 5-L1-1

Figure 5-L1-2

4. Cut circles, squares and rectangles freehand from the paper without drawing lines (Figure 5-L1-3).

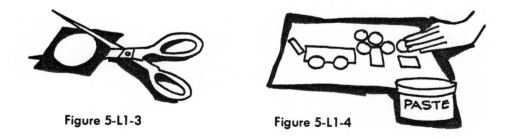

Figure 5-L1-3

Figure 5-L1-4

5. Arrange the various geometric shapes on the black construction paper base to create a realistic subject (Figures 5-L1-4).

6. Cut smaller shapes from the rest of the strips and add them as details to the subject. Paste the completed shapes into place.

7. Clean up! Replace unused paste in the jar. Save large, colored paper scraps. Wrap all other scraps in newspapers and throw them away. Wash up!

Variations:

1. For lower grades, cut one geometric shape and paste it on 12 × 18-inch manila paper. Use a crayon to draw a subject, using the geometric shape as part of the picture. A clown holding a balloon, a man standing on a box—or any other idea using the geometric shape as the basic element.

LESSON 2

Score One for the Fish!

Objectives:

1. To learn to score and fold paper.
2. To learn to create textures on a paper surface.
3. To create imaginative bulletin boards.

Materials:

18 × 24-inch, heavy (90 lb.) white paper, scissors, stencil knives, blue corrugated paper for a background, pencils, staplers, newspapers.

Guidelines:

Is that large blank bulletin board outside the classroom staring at you? Take the easy way out and fill it with a three-dimensional underwater scene that introduces a new art technique—scoring paper to change flat paper into a three-dimensional sculpture.

What kinds of fish shall you create? Sharks with big fins and teeth, a jellyfish with many tendrils suspended from its half-round body? If everyone selects a different fish to create, you'll have quite a variety of fish to staple to that blue paper background.

Draw the fish that you've selected on large white paper. It's easier to cut out large things and they usually look better. If you must correct your drawing, don't erase, merely draw over the error. Don't draw on both sides of the white paper, you must keep one side clean. What about fins for your fish? Draw them directly on the white paper. The fewer pieces added to the fish later, the better the final product. Better draw a circle for the eye of the fish; this can be cut out later.

Step back and take another look at your fish. Is everything in place? Cut around the outline of your fish. Save any surplus white paper for small details you may want to add later.

Now for the scoring of the paper fish. Using a pair of closed scissors, draw an imaginary line through the center of the fish. The heavy white paper will fold easily when pressed along this scored line and the beginning of a three-dimensional fish gradually emerges. Better have clean hands! White paper shows every line and smudge.

Now is the time to create textures in the surface of the paper and add more elaborate details such as teeth and eyes. It's always easier to cut away parts than add details piecemeal, so use scissors to cut into the fish shape. Use a sharp stencil knife to cut round or triangular slits in the paper surface to imitate scales. A thick pad of newspaper underneath will protect the desk from sharp knives. Lift these slits up from the paper with the stencil knife and scales are created! Gills, fins, and other details can also be cut more easily with a stencil knife than with a pair of scissors.

Look the completed fish over closely. Anything missing? Add whatever you want!

Mounting all the different kinds of fish on a bulletin board is easy. A few staples tacked in the tail and sides will readily hold them. Be sure to maintain that dimensional effect in the paper and avoid flattening out the fish when stapling them to the background. A nice blue crepe paper or corrugated paper background adds a lot!

How to Do It:

After a motivating discussion about various types of fish and undersea life:

1. Select the largest and heaviest-weight white paper available. Distribute stencil knives, scissors and paste, and spread newspapers to

protect the desk surface. Make certain that everyone washes his hands before beginning the activity.

2. Draw any type of fish on one side of the white paper. Fill the paper with a large drawing, adding fins, eyes, tails and other parts (Figure 5-L2-1).

3. Cut out the fish, in one piece (Figure 5-L1-2).

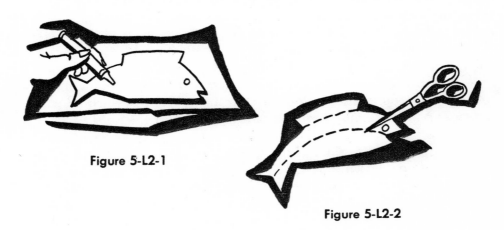

Figure 5-L2-1

Figure 5-L2-2

4. With the points of scissors in a closed position, score a line through the center of the paper fish. Fold the paper carefully on this scored line (Figure 5-L2-3).

5. Cut out eyes, textures and other details with stencil knives and scissors. Add any other small details (Figure 5-L2-4).

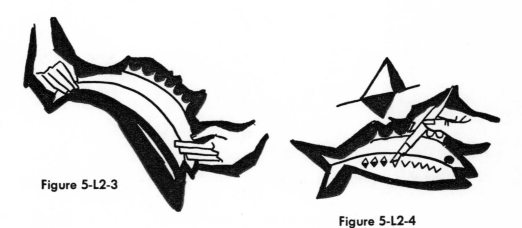

Figure 5-L2-3

Figure 5-L2-4

6. Staple corrugated paper, or crepe paper, over a bulletin board. Mount the different fishes on the bulletin board with a stapler. Add underwater vegetation to complete the scene (Figure 5-L2-5).

Figure 5-L2-5

7. Save large scraps of white paper. Roll the smaller scraps into the newspapers and throw them away. Wash up!

Variations:

1. Change the subject to people or animals and use the same process to create individual three-dimensional pictures.

LESSON 3

Tearing It Up!

Objectives:

1. To learn to create shapes by tearing paper.
2. To learn to overlap subjects and create depth in a picture.

Materials:

Colored construction paper, colored poster paper, a crayon, scissors, paper clips, school paste, paper towels, newspapers.

Guidelines:

Have you ever been so angry that you felt like tearing up things? If you have, then this activity is a sure cure. Tearing colored construction paper into shapes produces the quickest background for cut-paper pictures. No time wasted on drawing here—and the torn shapes look a lot more original too!

How about a torn-paper jungle? Think of all the tall grass, trees, bushes, and rivers you can tear into. What animals live in your jungle? Better cut these animals out with a pair of scissors after drawing them on colored paper. The smooth edges of the cut paper will contrast well with the rough torn paper. Select the easy animals, those that have "special" characteristics that stand out, like the mane of a lion—or a fat hippopotamus, large in head and body.

Want to make a herd of animals, or a pride of lions? Draw one animal carefully on poster-weight colored paper. Add a few sheets of similar paper under the drawing. Use a paper clip to hold these pieces of paper firmly together. One careful cut all around the animal and presto—a herd of giraffes! Need a lion to chase them? Just draw one and cut it out! Don't bother with little details on these animals. Add them later with a colored crayon.

Now for the jungle background to help our animals live in the right place. What do you need? A long grassy plain for the lions to feed in? Just tear a long strip of green paper. How about a watering hole torn out of blue paper—for your elephants to wallow in? Long strips of yellow-green paper create exotic jungle foliage. Lots of small scraps of colored paper are usable—for bushes, tree foliage—perhaps even a blazing sun.

Add a few details with a black crayon and your jungle comes to life!

How to Do It:

1. Prepare for pasting and cutting by covering the desks with newspapers, passing out paste, scissors, crayons, paper towels, and paper clips.

2. Place different colors of 12 × 18-inch construction paper and pieces of lighter-weight colored poster paper on a table. Have a box of scrap paper ready also.

3. Have pupils select their colors individually. A piece of colored construction paper for the base of the picture, scraps for tearing back-

ground shapes and a few pieces of poster-weight paper for cutting animal shapes.

4. Draw animal shapes on one piece of colored poster paper. Place several sheets of poster paper together and fasten them together with a paper clip. Cut the animals out of the layers of paper (Figures 5-L3-1 and 2).

Figure 5-L3-1

Figure 5-L3-2

5. Tear a variety of background shapes from scrap pieces of colored construction paper. Place the torn shapes on a background of colored construction paper (Figure 5-L3-3).

6. Overlap the cut-out animals over these background shapes on the base paper. Experiment with different arrangements and then paste the pieces into place when satisfied! Use a paper towel to remove paste from your fingers (Figure 5-L3-4).

Figure 5-L3-3

Figure 5-L3-4

7. Use a crayon to add interesting details to the picture (Figure 5-L3-5).

8. Clean up! Save the colored paper scraps for future lessons. Return unused paste to the jar and wash your hands.

Figure 5-L3-5

Variations:

1. Try tearing one large animal shape from colored construction paper. Mount this on a larger piece of colored paper and add all the details by tearing pieces of paper or drawing with a crayon.

LESSON 4

Under a Saran Sea!

Objectives:

1. To learn to overlap objects in a picture to create depth.

2. To learn to use combinations of different materials for dramatic effect.

Materials:

Colored construction paper, colored poster paper, scissors, school paste, a crayon, rolls of saran wrap, paper clips or staples, newspapers.

Guidelines:

Like to see through things? A trip to your local grocery store for a large roll of saran wrap will provide enough material to create transparencies that will allow you to see through everything! Combined with a few pieces of colored paper, scissors and a touch of crayon, you can create a whole ocean from one roll of saran wrap. Think of all the living things underwater that you can create. Seahorse or octopus, which shall you draw and cut out?

Begin by selecting a piece of blue or green construction paper to create upon. Color is important because saran wrap is transparent and all of the various colors underneath it will shimmer and ripple—just like the ocean itself!

Now for the fish that live in your ocean. Select pieces of colored paper that will contrast well against the blue or green base paper. How about a bright yellow for sharks? Will a pink jellyfish show up well against that dark blue base? What kinds of plants and coral can be cut out easily? Cut out all the various pieces and arrange them on your paper background.

Overlap as many denizens of the deep as possible because this adds the illusion of depth to your art. Cover it all with saran wrap and step back and enjoy it!

How to Do It:

1. Place a large box of saran wrap on a table in the front of the room.

2. Cover each desk with newspapers and distribute pieces of colored construction paper, scissors, paste, and a variety of colored scrap papers to each pupil. Have additional colored scrap paper available.

3. Use a crayon to draw a subject directly on a piece of colored paper (Figure 5-L4-1).

4. Add several other pieces of paper under the drawing, fastening them together with paper clips or a stapler. Use a pair of scissors to cut out several shapes simultaneously (Figure 5-L4-2).

Figure 5-L4-1

Figure 5-L4-2

5. Experiment arranging these cut shapes and other shapes on a background paper. Paste into place when satisfied (Figure 5-L4-3).

6. Use crayons to add small drawing details to the cut-paper shapes (Figure 5-L4-4).

7. Carry the completed underwater scene to the table containing saran wrap. Pull a piece of saran wrap over the completed picture. Cut

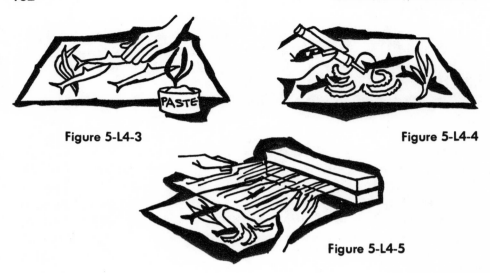

Figure 5-L4-3   **Figure 5-L4-4**

Figure 5-L4-5

the saran wrap with scissors or the cutting edge of the box. Use the palm of your hand to press the saran wrap to paper. Trim off any excess saran wrap with a pair of scissors (Figure 5-L4-5).

Clean up by throwing away small scraps. Save larger pieces of colored paper for the scrap box. Return unused paste to the jar and wash up. Save the saran wrap for other activities.

Variations:

1. Press paper shapes directly on a piece of saran wrap without using a base paper. Press this completed piece to a classroom window. Instant holiday displays!

LESSON 5

Fold It and Dye!

Objectives:

1. To learn techniques of dyeing materials.

2. To learn to create repetitive patterns through folding paper in various ways.

Materials:

Cold-water dyes, absorbent paper towels, large plastic bowls, large pitchers of water, newspapers.

Guidelines:

Those television commercials that praise the absorbent strength of various types of paper toweling are right on target! This particular characteristic of paper towels can be lots of fun and useful when combined with a few bright-colored, cold-water dyes. Watch the paper soak up the color! A roll of absorbent paper towels will produce a myriad of brilliantly colored patterns for you.

You can create a variety of different designs through folding paper toweling into various shapes and then dipping the corners of these folded papers into different colors of dye. Since this is a brief activity, you will be able to create many different designs.

Experiment first, several days ahead, with one sheet of absorbent paper toweling, several water color cups and liquid food dyes or other cold-water dyes. Cold-water dyes tend to be less intense when thinned too much with water, so a little experimenting with proportions is in order. Your tests will provide some idea of how much dye to mix into larger amounts of cold water. Don't wait until the day of the activity to experiment!

You can lead the folding of the paper toweling "by the numbers." Any creativity that is going to occur will follow the first few tentative attempts at dyeing. You'll find your own "thing" easily after you learn how to do it.

How to Do It:

1. Organize the class to work in small groups. Protect all desk surfaces with a thick layer of newspapers. Wear old shirts to protect clothes.

2. Mix cold-water dyes in watercolor cups according to instructions on the box. Distribute two dye colors and several sheets of paper toweling to each group of pupils (Figure 5-L5-1).

3. Fold paper towels into various shapes: squares, triangles, and rectangles (Figure 5-L5-2).

Figure 5-L5-1

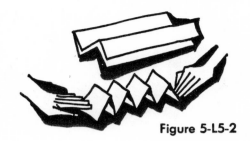

Figure 5-L5-2

4. Dip the corners of the folded paper into various dye colors to create different color patterns (Figure 5-L5-3).

5. Open the folded paper and use a large blotter to absorb any excess dampness. Repeat the dyeing process, using a variety of folds (Figure 5-L5-4).

Figure 5-L5-3

Figure 5-L5-4

6. Clean up! Empty dyes into a sink and run cold water for a minute to wash the dyes down the drain. If you have white enameled sinks, empty the dyes into the earth outside. Throw away newspapers and wash up!

Variations:

1. After pupils have learned the process of dyeing, cloth can be substituted for paper and each pupil can create his own scarf.

LESSON 6

Creating Flowers That Move!

Objectives:

1. To learn to create dimensionally using flat paper.

2. To learn to work in groups on one theme or subject.

Materials:

Colored construction paper, scissors, hand staplers and staples, pipe cleaners, large rolls of construction paper, school paste, newspapers.

Guidelines:

You can use all the skills you've learned about cutting through several layers of paper to create moving flowers for a mural. All you need are lots of busy hands, lots of interest and a bulletin board to fill.

Have you noticed that the shapes of petals on different flowers vary greatly? Which flower are you most familiar with? If you can draw a petal of this flower all you need to do is place other pieces of paper underneath your drawing and you're in the business of mural-making.

Start thinking about a "spring thing" because your bulletin board mural will soon be filled with cut-paper flowers stapled to flexible pipe cleaner stems that move when touched by hands or the wind. What else can you add to extend the theme of spring? How about some interesting people? Put your best artists to work on a large figure for your paper mural. The flowers will soon be ready to be picked!

You can paste or staple flowers together, all depending upon what tools are on hand. It's a little more difficult to staple the many small pieces together, but pupils love to use staplers. You'll need an extra center to hide the metal staples. Two long pipe cleaners twisted together create a stem. Staple the stem to your flower and you have created one of the many pieces you'll need to complete your spring mural.

How to Do It:

After motivating pupils to create a spring scene:

1. Organize the class into small groups to share materials and to work on various parts of the mural. Distribute scissors, staplers, school paste, pipe cleaners and cover desks with newspapers.

2. Allow pupils to select colors for their subjects from construction paper placed on a table.

3. Begin by drawing one petal of a flower and cutting it from colored paper (Figure 5-L6-1).

4. Fold colored construction paper into two or four folds. Trace

Figure 5-L6-1   **Figure 5-L6-2**

the already completed petal on the folded paper and cut out several petals simultaneously (Figure 5-L6-2).

5. Arrange the cut flower petals around a center cut from colored construction paper. Fasten each petal in position using a hand stapler or paste.

6. Staple a stem made from two pipe cleaners twisted together. Staple this to the flower and cover the stapled center with another circle (Figure 5-L6-3).

7. Staple the flowers onto a bulletin board to create a spring scene. Add cut paper figures and details created by other pupils (Figure 5-L6-4).

Figure 5-L6-3

Figure 5-L6-4

8. Clean up by throwing away all small scraps of colored paper. Organize extra pipe cleaners by wrapping one pipe cleaner tightly around the others. Wash up!

Variations:

1. Once the class has learned to create flowers, motivate them to

invent an original flower, such as: people-eating flowers, sky-raising flowers, underground flowers or even animal flowers!

LESSON 7

Box Your Subject!

Objectives:

1. To learn to create dioramas.
2. To learn about the elements of depth and overlapping.

Materials:

Shoe boxes or round hat boxes, saran wrap, colored construction paper, oak tag, scissors, materials from nature, black tempera paint, large watercolor brushes, paste, newspapers.

Guidelines:

Don't throw those old shoe boxes away; there may be a better use for them. With just a few scrap pieces of oak tag, colored construction paper, paint and a box of saran wrap, you can turn those boxes into three-dimensional dioramas!

The sky's the limit! Looking for a different idea for the coming holiday? Dioramas are it! Any celebration from Hallowe'en to Christmas is possible using simple paper techniques and a little originality. Once you have selected the right holiday to celebrate in a diorama, begin thinking about materials. Are there any small objects around the room that might add another dimension to the cut-paper figures you are going to make? How about looking to nature? Those milkweed pods have just the feathery touch to help that Hallowe'en ghost appear a bit more mysterious. A few small twigs from a tree will add a realistic, tiny "tree" to the diorama about George Washington. What else will fit in the shoe box? It will be hard to place anything heavy or large in that small space. Think it over; let those ideas germinate—and don't forget to begin collecting boxes!

Those paper figures you've cut need propping up. Fold tabs of oak tag and paste them to the bottom of the figures. Move the figures around in the box in different positions until they overlap other objects, then paste them into place. Now is the time to add the small touches that make the difference! A colored pipe cleaner may be just the thing for a ghostly jump rope, or perhaps some colored tissue paper pasted to the top of the box will hand down in eerie folds. Break open that milkweed pod you saved, add a few twigs with a bit of glue, and presto! A Hallowe'en diorama!

How to Do It:

After discussing and motivating a holiday theme:

1. Begin by collecting shoe boxes and other scrap materials before beginning the activity.

2. Prepare desks with newspapers before painting the boxes with tempera paint. Set aside an area for the painted boxes to dry so that they will not clutter up the desks (Figure 5-L7-1).

Figure 5-L7-1

Figure 5-L7-2

3. Draw diorama figures directly on construction paper and cut them out. Make several different figures (Figure 5-L7-2).

4. Add details to the cut-out figures wtih colored construction paper and paste, or use crayons to create eyes and other small details.

5. Cut tabs from oak tag, fold them, and paste one side to the bottom of the cut-out figures so that the figures "stand up" (Figure 5-L7-3).

6. Experiment in placing the cut-out figures and other materials in the painted shoe box. Paste them into position. Use white glue for objects such as twigs, stones and sand (Figure 5-L7-4).

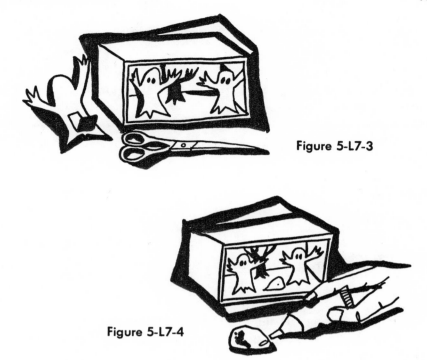

Figure 5-L7-3

Figure 5-L7-4

7. Stretch saran wrap over the front of the box and press it into place firmly (Figure 5-L7-5).

Figure 5-L7-5

8. Clean up by piling the scraps on top of the newspapers, rolling them into small bundles and throwing them away. Wash the brushes in water and return unused materials to the closet and scrap box. Throw away the natural materials. They may spoil!

Variations:

1. Organize small groups to work on slightly larger dioramas of hatbox size. Make everything larger. Try correlating with social studies—a cut-away view of a coal mine, or an era of history.

LESSON 8
Making Funny Faces

Objectives:

1. To learn to create three-dimensionally.
2. To learn to attach various types of materials to basic shapes.
3. To use imagination in creating original masks.

Materials:

Heavy manila oak tag (150 lb. stock), scissors, colored construction paper, paste or white glue, newspapers, miscellaneous small objects.

Guidelines:

Looking for something unusual to do on those rainy days that seem to hang heavy on your hands! It takes a lot of excitement to shake the doldrums—and creating original masks is just the trick!

Making imaginary heads is not a strain on the brain since anything goes. Want to make a one-eyed monster? Go right ahead! The only limitation upon your imagination is the number and different types of materials available. The more the merrier! Collect as many different materials and objects as you can; who knows what you will want to add as you create your own original mask? Objects such as large buttons, rickrack, yarn, fringes, felt and old false eyelashes will all serve to add dimension to flat paper materials. And dimension is what makes the mask more realistic!

You'll need a partner to complete several phases of this activity. It is difficult to staple the basic cylinder without assistance. A partner will also prove helpful to locate and mark the eyes in the completed cylinder.

Use school paste or white glue to add all the elaborate details you desire. Use construction paper to create more depth on your basic mask. Curl, score, fold paper details to create more dimension.

140

How to Do It:

After discussing imaginary animals and masks:

1. Pre-cut heavy oak tag into 15 × 30-inch pieces.

2. Distribute scissors, crayons, and other materials to the class. Provide white glue, paste and a stapler for each group of pupils. Cover tables with newspapers.

3. Roll the pre-cut oak tag pieces into a cylinder. Use a partner to hold the oak tag while stapling each end of the cylinder (Figure 5-L8-1).

4. Place the cylinder over your head using a partner to mark the location of your eyes with a crayon (Figure 5-L8-2). Draw a circle for each eye around the crayon mark. After removing the mask from the head, use a scissors to pierce through the oak tag and cut out the eyes (Figure 5-L8-3).

5. Add three-dimensional parts to the head using a variety of materials. Use white glue for heavier materials, and paste for the paper pieces that are added to the mask (Figure 5-L8-4).

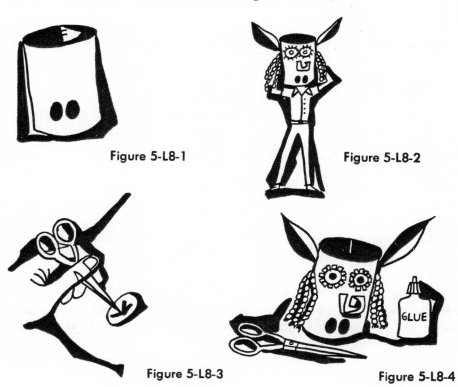

Figure 5-L8-1

Figure 5-L8-2

Figure 5-L8-3

Figure 5-L8-4

6. Throw away all small scraps. Save the remaining paste and large scraps of material for a scrap box. Wash up!

Variations:

1. For lower grades, use the same methods to create an oak tag cylinder and add all the details with tempera paint and brush.

LESSON 9

Save the Boxes!

Objectives:

1. To learn to create three-dimensional objects using scrap materials.

2. To stimulate imagination through the use of various materials.

Materials:

A variety of boxes of various sizes, colored construction paper, pipe cleaners, buttons, "found" materials, white glue, school paste, scissors, rug yarn, tempera paint, watercolor brushes, newspapers.

Guidelines:

Have you looked around in your garage or attic lately? Stored away in these little-traveled areas are a wealth of materials, ready to go to work. Begin with boxes—any kind of boxes, from large corrugated ones to tiny, old-fashioned pill boxes. You'll never know which boxes will be the most useful.

That long thin box, and the round box next to it may be just the thing to construct a giraffe. Those small boxes *already* look like bugs! It won't take much to turn them into ladybugs or spiders! With a little bright tempera paint and pipe cleaners for legs they'll look just right. Oh! Look at what's inside this box—buttons! They will look just like eyes when adhered with a bit of white glue.

That round oatmeal box over there will make a stand-up bunny. All you need is a stapler to "tack" the pipe cleaner whisers on, plus a little paint and colored paper for those big rabbit ears!

You don't need many materials to transform a few boxes into a roaring lion or a timid rabbit. A bit of paste or white glue for applying colored paper, and staplers for attaching small details are necessary. You will need some white glue to adhere slightly heavier materials, such as buttons, rug yarn or cloth to the boxes. A roll of masking tape will help to hold any materials that cannot be pasted or stapled to the boxes.

How to Do It:

1. Collect boxes of various shapes and sizes. Place them in a corner of the room and let ideas generate! On the day of the lesson, have individual pupils select those boxes they think they will need to create imaginary animals.

2. Distribute paste, white glue, staplers, newspapers, colored paper, and other materials to groups of pupils. Cover the desks with newspapers. Miscellaneous colored paper and small scraps of other material should be readily available for individuals to use when needed.

3. Use white glue to adhere boxes and combine them into an animal shape. Apply glue to the surfaces of both boxes (Figure 5-L9-1).

4. While the boxes are drying, cut other materials into shapes that can be used later. Glue, or paste these shapes into position on the boxes when the glue is fairly dry (Figure 5-L9-2).

Figure 5-L9-1

Figure 5-L9-2

Figure 5-L9-3

5. Add other dimensional materials to the animal, using white glue or a stapler (Figure 5-L9-3).

6. Cut out paper designs, or paint designs, on the completed animal shape.

7. Clean up! Throw away small scraps in the newspapers. Save three-dimensional materials and large scraps of paper for a collage lesson. Wash up!

Variations:

1. Organize pupils into groups of three to help shorten the activity time. Use tempera paint for most details, adding yarn or other materials to the surface when the paint is dry.

LESSON 10

Weaving Through the Warp!

Objectives:

To learn the basic techniques of weaving.

2. To develop an awareness of the art of weaving and its function in society.

Materials:

12 × 18-inch colored construction paper, rulers, scissors, stapler and staples, a pencil.

Guidelines:

You can learn a lot about weaving before attempting to warp in your own pattern on a real loom. Weaving begins with simple over-and-under movements through a "warp," which is the strands of thread or yarn tautly stretched between ends of a loom. All this is easy to imitate using common colored construction paper for both the warp and "weft"—the lines going the other way.

The pattern that you use in paper weaving cannot be too complicated, even if you desire it so. But it is possible to cut some pretty, curved lines to create the "warp" part of your paper weaving. Select strongly contrasting colors for both warp and weft, making it easy to follow the simple over-and-under pattern as it develops.

You can vary the warp pattern by drawing curves and other irregular lines on paper. Later on you can vary both warp and weft patterns in widths, colors, curves or straight lines. All these variations will help to make each paper weaving project a little bit different.

Try weaving paper more than one time. In your first experience you're merely learning how to do it and thinking is somewhat secondary. You can weave pretty fancy once you have experienced the basic fundamentals of paper weaving.

How to Do It:

1. Distribute rulers, scissors, crayons and hand staplers to small groups of pupils.

2. Arrange a variety of pieces of 12 × 18-inch colored construction paper at a table in the classroom. Pupils may select two pieces of contrasting colors, one for the warp and the other to cut as weft.

3. Use a pencil and ruler to draw a line one inch down from the paper's edge and across the 12-inch width of the colored paper selected for the "warp" (Figure 5-L10-1).

Figure 5-L10-1

4. Draw lines the length of the same paper, ending at the drawn line. These may be curved, vary in width, or be drawn as straight lines of all the same width (Figure 5-L10-2).

5. Use scissors to cut these lines up to the mark (Figure 5-L10-3).

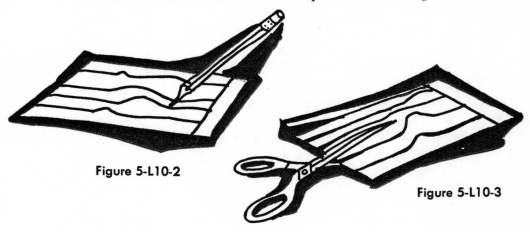

Figure 5-L10-2

Figure 5-L10-3

6. Cut contrasting pieces of colored paper for the weft completely across the 12-inch width of a 12 × 18-inch piece of construction paper. These strips may vary in width and shape. Use a ruler to mark the lines if straight strips are desired.

7. Demonstrate weaving the contrasting-colored weft strip over and under each warp strip. Start each alternating weft strip the opposite of the previous strip; that is, if the first weft strip went *under* the first warp strip, the next weft strip should start *over* the next warp strip (Figure 5-L10-4).

Figure 5-L10-4

8. Use a stapler, or paste, to secure the final weft strip into place. This is necessary to hold all the woven paper strips in place.

9. Clean up by returning scissors and rulers to place and wash up.

Variations:

1. Create your own loom from a picture frame and weave rug yarn.

CHAPTER 6

Working with Wood

INTRODUCTION TO WOOD

Wood is frequently overlooked as an art medium in elementary school classrooms because some tools and materials are not readily available. Yet, these same tools and materials are resting, unused, in garages, attics and cellars. With a little organized collecting, your class can have all the hammers, wood scraps and nails you will need. The effort and time spent collecting materials will be satisfying once you observe the intense concentration of young children drilling and hammering away at wood.

Some simple wood activities don't even require special tools. Scrap-wood sculpture can easily be assembled using a fast-setting cement. But children are capable of learning to hammer nails at an early age, if you begin by using nails with large heads. Gradually introduce drilling into wood and fastening wood pieces together using méta' screws, until students become secure and competent using tools.

There are several different types of wood that will become visible in your scrap box. It is impossible to predict what kinds of wood children will bring to school. Hardwood, such as maple, oak, and fir, is difficult for children to hammer nails into. Other woods, such as pine, tend to split when nailed. Thick pieces of plywood accept nails without splitting because plywood is composed of several different layers of wood. Try any nailing activity you have planned for the class yourself before introducing it to children. This will help to identify any problem areas using tools and materials.

Wood is a manipulative material that suggests many various

dimensions and spatial compositions to three-dimensionally-oriented children. Even greater aesthetic depths can be reached in decorating and finishing the wood sculpture. There is a wealth of art to be explored, using wood.

Wood Tools and Materials

To explore the gamut of wood activities a variety of tools are necessary; hammers, screw drivers and twist drills. These tools are used in conjunction with nails, wood screws and drill bits to help join various pieces of wood together. Not all activities using wood require individual tools for each pupil. Tools can be shared in both individual and group activities.

Whenever it is necessary to use hammers and nails in an activity, try to plan the lessons early or late in the school year when the class can work outside. Mother Earth can more readily absorb the blows of hammers and sharp-pointed nails than classroom desks.

Wood activities become more flexible for younger artists if many small pieces of wood are cut in a great variety of sizes and shapes. This can be accomplished using a simple electrical "bayonet" saw or, if you are lucky enough to have a friend with a hobby, a table jig saw. Variety is the key to success. Cut the small wood pieces into curves, rectangles, long strips, short strips, triangles or combinations of all these shapes. Save all of the small pieces in a large cardboard box until you have enough for a class activity. Each pupil may use from 10 to 16 small pieces of wood in an average assemblage.

White wood glue is the best adhesive to use with elementary age pupils, despite its slow-drying characteristic. Any wood assemblage activity can be finished in a shorter time, if contact cement is substituted for white glue. You cannot correct mistakes as easily, however. Be prepared to throw away old brushes after you have used them with fast-drying contact cement. Use white glue liberally and contact cement sparingly.

Organizing for Wood Activities

Some wood activities should be individually oriented; other activities are best suited for small groups of three to four pupils. Working with large wood sculpture is quite similar to group activities in making murals. All pupils need to become involved in activities they understand and can accomplish. Give some thought to organizing each small group to provide students of various skills and abilities. Not all pupils who draw and paint well will prove to be the best three-dimensional artists, though some will. Become aware of your pupils' strengths in both two- and three-dimensional art activities.

Hammering is a physical activity. It is best accomplished outside the classroom and school on soft ground. There are several reasons, exclusive of creating nail holes in classroom desks, for holding nailing activities in an outside environment: (1) pupils have more space to hammer and create in; (2) small groups have ample room to work safely with swinging hammers, and; (3) there is a certain ambience when creating in an outside environment, away from the classroom. A certain freedom exists.

Wood sculptures and assemblages are sometimes improved through changing their surfaces. A great variety of surface treatments can be accomplished in an elementary classroom. Wood can be varnished, stained, painted with acrylic or tempera paint, or sprayed with enamel paint cans. Some wood pieces seem to "ask" for surface design, others need simple transparent finishes. If the sculpture is to be located outside, exterior type paints and varnishes must be used.

Common Problems Using Wood

As in all art activities, experience with the material used raises or lowers the level of creative expectation. All beginning wood experiences should be kept simple and exploratory until pupils gain confidence and security using the medium.

Hammering nails into wood is a natural physical activity that pupils of young ages are capable of and enjoy. Hammering nails to fasten two pieces of wood together is a bit more difficult. Screwing two pieces of wood together is even more difficult. There are various levels of difficulty encountered in fastening wood together. Test these various limitations through selecting several pupils to explore the activity, prior to initiating it with the total group.

When using nails or wood screws in soft wood such as pine, rub each nail or screw over a piece of soap. Adding soft soap to the metal permits it to penetrate the wood fibers with less resistance, eliminating the problem of splitting. Pupils need a lot of instruction and supervision in hammering and drilling wood. There is a tendency for the more physically mature pupils to "take over" in small group activities, excluding other pupils from full involvement. Observe small groups of pupils at work and be ready to make suggestions to keep all pupils fully involved. There are tasks for all levels and skills in working with wood.

When using wood finishes such as stains, shellac, or varnish, be certain that windows are kept open to provide adequate ventilation. Odors in close classrooms are a problem.

Storage of pupil work can become a problem if wood activities extend over several periods and days. Three-dimensional art work does require more storage space than other activities. Sometimes, additional storage space can be created by stacking similar size corrugated cardboard boxes in a corner of the classroom. These homemade containers will store quite a few pupil projects.

DEVELOPMENTAL CHART OF WOOD ACTIVITIES

WOOD ACTIVITY (GRADE LEVEL)	NEW MATERIALS INTRODUCED	PHYSICAL SKILLS INVOLVED	PUPILS LEARN	EMOTIONAL AND INTELLECTUAL EXPERIENCES
Glue It, Then Paint It (Wood Assemblage) (K-3)	Small pre-cut scraps of wood White glue Magic markers Use of bases	Holding pieces in place for drying. Applying white glue. Drawing with felt-tip pens.	That wood scraps can create a variety of shapes. To glue wood and paper. To add line and color to three-dimensional art.	Touching Assembling Inventing
Pictures Get Framed (Decoupage) (3-6)	Shellac Varnish Old pictures Large nails Hammer	Painting with shellac. Hammering nails and wood. Gluing paper to wood.	To use varnish and shellac. To use a hammer and nails.	Experimenting Arranging
Lollipops Stick-Up (Lollipop Sculpture) (5-6)	Lollipop sticks Duco cement	Holding small pieces for gluing. Creating modular shapes of triangles and squares with toothpicks.	To create open-spaced sculpture. That modular construction works with similar size pieces.	Visualizing Assembling Creating
Building Balsa Up (Balsa Sculpture) (5-6)	Balsa wood Duco cement Pins Stencil knives	Cutting with stencil knives. Gluing and pinning balsa pieces together. Painting wood surfaces.	To vary space and lines created with balsa wood. Techniques in adhering soft wood.	Arranging Assembling Deciding
Box That Sculpture (3-6)	Cigar boxes White glue Small scrap wood	Gluing and placing wood within a limited space.	To create sculpture within a confined area by varying space and height.	Arranging Selecting
Start With Broomsticks (Wood scrap and broomstick sculpture) (5-6)	Large scrap wood Nails Hand drills	Working in groups with a single wooden base. Drilling into wood. Nailing wood together.	To plan together in creating large sculpture. To use hand tools. To create design in space.	Assembling Composing Investing
Flexible Shapes (5-6)	Reed or cane Duco cement	Holding and gluing wood. Bending and shaping material.	To create shapes using flexible materials. To glue various types of wood together. To create spatially.	Assembling Constructing Estimating Measuring
Wood Photo Cubes (Photographs Glued to Wood) (4-6)	Photographs, or pictures from magazines	Gluing Trimming	To create with found materials. To overlap materials creating simple design.	Selecting Measuring Deciding
Alphabet Jewelry (5-6)	Tongue depressors Alphabet soup letters	Gluing and cutting small materials.	To create functional objects from scraps.	Creating Arranging Designing

Glue It, Then Paint It!

Objectives:

1. To learn to assemble and construct three-dimensional sculpture.

2. To develop the ability to work spontaneously and intuitively with spatial relationships.

Materials:

Small wood scraps of various sizes and shapes, masonite or plywood pieces for use as a base; white glue, tempera paint, small water color brushes, watercolor cups, Magic Markers or crayons, newspapers.

Guidelines:

If you've never experienced the happy task of gluing and arranging small bits of scrap wood to construct a design "in the round," then get ready to enjoy yourself, It *is* fun to manipulate wooden shapes, arranging different clusters of pieces, trying out various compositions, and finally deciding upon the most satisfactory one. This is where basic learning about sculpture begins—with simple, but visually effective, processes used in the creation of scrap-wood sculpture.

Better start collecting as much scrap wood as possible right away! You'll find, as the wood starts coming in, that you will need a large box, or plastic bags to store it. Since "beggars can't be choosers" you will probably find some of the wood out-size, or too large to work with. Some friend with a power saw can soon remedy this problem!

Keep your eyes open for pieces of plywood or masonite to use as the foundation for your wood sculpture. Corrugated cardboard can be substituted for wood although the material tends to "curl" a bit if glue is used excessively.

How to Do It:

1. Begin collecting wood scrap pieces at least one week before the lesson. Encourage pupils to bring in small pieces of wood already

pre-cut. This will save time and effort. Store the collected wood in large corrugated boxes, or strong plastic bags, until ready for use.

2. Organize the class into groups of four to six pupils. If tables are not available, push desks together to create a larger work area. Protect the desks or tables with a layer of newspapers.

3. Distribute all the materials to each group: pieces for the base, handfuls of small scrap-wood pieces and white glue.

4. Encourage pupils to "try out" various arrangements with the wood scraps. Stress variety of size and shapes through demonstrating. Once the arrangement is completed, glue the wood scraps on the base piece (Figure 6-L1-1).

Figure 6-L1-1

5. Place the completed pieces in a safe location to dry. Avoid touching or moving the sculpture during the drying time (about 2 hours).

6. The second phase of this activity can begin anytime after the sculpture is dry. Distribute brushes, tempera paint, water, enameled water cups, and crayons or magic markers.

7. If crayons instead of Magic Markers are used for designs, show the class a variety of textural lines such as straight, wiggly or polka dots. Thinned tempera paint can be applied over these lines to provide more background color (Figure 6-L1-2).

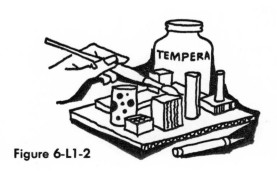

Figure 6-L1-2

Figure 6-L1-3

8. If Magic Markers are used instead of crayons, the tempera colors are painted on first and allowed to dry before lines are drawn on with Magic Markers (Figure 6-L1-3).

9. Place the completed sculpture in a safe location to dry.

10. Clean up by washing out brushes and paint cups, replacing caps on the bottles of white glue, and throwing away all scraps of paper. Save usable wood pieces in a scrap box.

Variations:

1. Use colored construction paper on some sides of the wood scraps instead of painting with tempera. This technique will accelerate the completion time of the lesson.

2. Substitute cut out photographs and pictures from magazines, gluing these on *some* sides of the wood scraps.

LESSON 2

Pictures Get Framed

Objectives:

1. To learn the art of decoupage.

2. To learn to use a combination of unusual materials to create art.

Materials:

Pieces of soft wood, a pre-selected picture or painting from a magazine, white glue, shellac, denatured alcohol, old brushes or clean rags to apply shellac; hammers or heavy metal objects, a few nails with large heads, newspapers, scissors, screw eyes to hang the completed decoupage.

Guidelines:

Although the word decoupage itself sounds pretty fancy, the decoupage process is a fairly old and simple one. It simply refers to mounting a picture on a wood panel. Take a little time and thought when selecting your favorite painting or picture to use in a decoupage. Once it is glued into place on top of distressed wood the design is very permanent.

Lucky are you, if you find a lengthy piece of soft pine or plywood that can be cut into several pieces, for you'll need a large-size piece of wood for each decoupage. Although specific sizes are pretty flexible, you'd better not select too large a picture since you'll need an even larger piece of wood to frame it. There should be a margin of wood remaining around each picture to act as a frame. Part of the joy in creating a decoupage is whacking away with a hammer at the pine to "distress" the soft wood surface. Add a few well-spaced holes along the wooden margin with a hammer and nail and everything is ready for antiquing your favorite picture with shellac.

In case you haven't noticed, shellac has an odor. Better open a few windows to air out your working area, or better yet why not create the final step (shellacking) outside?

How to Do It:

1. Explain decoupage to the class. Show a sample, if possible.

2. Select a photograph as a subject and select a piece of soft pine a few inches larger than the photograph. Use scissors to trim the photograph to fit within the perimeter of the wood (Figure 6-L2-1).

Figure 6-L2-1

3. Organize the class into groups of four pupils each and cover their tables with newspapers. Distribute two or more hammers and a few large nails to each group.

4. Place the trimmed picture on the wood. Trace around the picture to mark the outline. All holes and distressing are done outside this perimeter (Figure 6-L2-2).

5. Demonstrate hammering holes into the wood, using large nails with heads. Explain that a few heavy taps will create holes in the surface, but one heavy blow may split the wood (Figure 6-L2-3).

Figure 6-L2-2

Figure 6-L2-3

6. Use any type of hammer or heavy metal object to further distress the wood around the perimeter of the picture (Figure 6-L2-4).

7. Use white glue to adhere the picture to the surface of the wood within the penciled outline (Figure 6-L2-5).

8. Once the glue has dried (in about one hour) apply orange shellac or decoupage liquid over the entire surface, using an old brush or clean rags (Figure 6-L2-6).

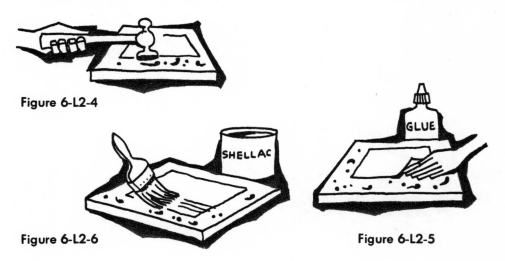

Figure 6-L2-4

Figure 6-L2-6

Figure 6-L2-5

9. Clean brushes in denatured alcohol and set outside in the air to dry. Throw *all* papers and extra materials away outside; do not keep them in the classroom. Return all tools to their proper location. Save excess wood pieces for future activities.

Variations:

1. Use a large scrap piece of plywood as a base for a group decoupage activity. Hang this in the school hallway.

2. Add screw eyes and picture wire to the back of each individual decoupage to facilitate hanging the completed piece.

LESSON 3

Lollipops Stick Up!

Objectives:

1. To learn to create modular designs using three-dimensional materials.

2. To develop an awareness of the relationships between spaces in "open" types of sculpture.

Materials:

Lollipop or medical swab sticks, Duco cement, corrugated cardboard, scissors, newspapers.

Guidelines:

Want to create a "skybreaker" or perhaps merely a meandering piece of sculpture? Lollipop or medical swab sticks, available at your local drug store, are the answer to your prayers. Both types of sticks can be purchased inexpensively in bulk quantities. It takes about two or three boxes of 500 sticks to be completely ready for this activity. You never know when some budding Michelangelo will get carried away and want to create a 15-foot high sculpture!

Patience and fortitude are the required ingredients when sculpturing with lollipop sticks. Although round toothpicks can be substituted for the longer lollipop or swab sticks, the shorter toothpicks add considerable time to the activity. It takes anywhere from two to three hours to complete a small wood sculptural piece a foot high, even with the longer lollipop sticks. But this activity seems to demand your attention and one soon gets caught up in gluing additions to the growing sculpture.

Better not attempt lollipop sculpture unless fast-drying glues are available. Duco cement is the least expensive of this type of adhesive and is readily available in tubes that pupils can easily share. Contact cement, of the type used by cabinet makers, is even faster and four pupils can share small cans of contact cement by dipping the sticks into the glue or using old brushes. The faster it dries, the faster the sculpture grows!

How to Do It:

1. Purchase inexpensive lollipop sticks, medical swab sticks or toothpicks, prior to beginning the activity. Using large scissors, pre-cut corrugated cardboard bases for each pupil (Figure 6-L3-1).

2. Organize the class into small groups of four pupils each. Distribute to each group: a handful of sticks, two tubes of fast-drying glue, newspapers for covering the tables. Partners can work together to create one sculpture or may create individual pieces.

3. Begin the sculpture by gluing sticks in a square or triangular shape, to the base (Figure 6-L3-2).

Figure 6-L3-1   Figure 6-L3-2

4. Add more sticks to the construction, using Duco cement to build up from the base. Hold the sticks together with fingers until they are fairly dry (Figure 6-L3-3).

Figure 6-L3-3   **Figure 6-L3-4**

5. Stick sculpture is extended outwardly by building more modules from the sides of the basic piece.

6. Additional sticks may be added *across* the growing sculpture to extend shapes in different directions (Figure 6-L3-4).

Variations:

1. Glue pieces of bright-colored tissue paper, or colored cellophane, over some of the modular shapes created by the sticks.

2. Combine several sculptures together on a table to create a larger sculpture. Think of titles for the sculptural pieces.

LESSON 4

Building Balsa Up!

Objectives:

1. To learn to construct three-dimensional art using soft woods and glue.

2. To learn to create original three-dimensional sculpture.

Materials:

Balsa sticks of various lengths and widths, tubes of Duco (or any fast-drying) cement, stencil knives, common pins, pieces of cardboard for bases, colored cellophane, newspapers.

Guidelines:

The sky is the limit when you use strips of balsa wood to construct sculpture, since you can attain pretty fair heights in no time at all. It's the extra length (balsa is sold in lengths of 36 inches) that offers an opportunity to create a simple open type of sculpture that can soar in any direction. Talk about flexibility!

You'll need an extra hand, as well as a small handful of common pins, so pick yourself a partner. He'll come in handy when it comes time to hold pieces while pinning them together, and also to help make decisions about the shapes of the open areas created by the balsa strips. All you need to make your partnership complete are a few strips of 1/4-inch or 1/8-inch square balsa wood, Duco cement, pins and stencil knives. If you want to add a bit of color, glue colored cellophane over some of the open areas. Another option is a base for the sculpture. A well-balanced balsa sculpture will stand alone without a base, but if you feel you need a base, use a large piece of corrugated cardboard. A base makes it a bit easier to pick up your piece of sculpture and carry it without damaging it. Balsa is fragile and the less rough handling it receives, the longer your art will last.

Better test any cements before you use them. Some cements do not harden quickly enough to be functional in a classroom situation and others are absorbed into the soft wood, losing their adhesive quality. Duco cement or contact cement are both fast-setting types of adhesives that conveniently come in easy-to-use handy tubes.

How to Do It:

1. Organize the class into small groups of two or three pupils each. Use newspapers to protect tables or desks pushed together to create a larger work area. Pre-cut 18 × 24-inch square pieces of corrugated cardboard for use as a base (optional).

2. Distribute a tube of cement, several 1/4- and 1/8-inch square pieces of balsa wood, one pre-cut corrugated cardboard base, a stencil knife and common pins to each group. Reserve other pieces of balsa wood at a table where pupils can select what they need.

3. Begin the construction by creating a basic "upward" shape using the 1/4-inch square pieces of balsa wood. Apply fast-drying cement to all pieces of balsa that touch. Pins can be used to reinforce some joints temporarily (Figure 6-L4-1).

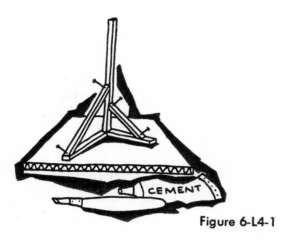

Figure 6-L4-1

Figure 6-L4-2

4. Add other pieces of balsa at any angle, *across* the basic shape extending the sculpture outwardly. Pin these or hold until dry (Figure 6-L4-2).

5. Continue to build and add smaller-dimension balsa pieces to the sculpture until it is completed. Emphasize different lengths, shapes and angles. Try to avoid creating simple squares and triangles.

6. Apply Duco cement to each balsa wood joint. Allow time for drying and remove any reinforcing pins very carefully (Figure 6-L4-3).

7. Paint the entire sculpture using black tempera paint and a small brush, or cut pieces of colored cellophane and adhere these over some of the open shapes created (optional). (Figure 6-L4-4.)

8. Clean up by throwing away small scraps, replace caps on the tubes of cement and save balsa wood scraps for other activities.

Figure 6-L4-3

Figure 6-L4-4

Variations:

1. Hang small objects on the balsa sculpture to celebrate holidays such as Christmas, Saint Valentine's Day, etc.

2. Place the sculpture in front of the window. Observe and discuss the shadows it casts and the colored light passing through the colored cellophane.

LESSON 5

Box That Sculpture!

Objectives:

1. To solve the problem of using three-dimensional shapes within limited space.

2. To develop a sense of awareness of textural sculpture.

Materials:

Small scraps of wood varying in height and width, small wooden boxes (cigar boxes are excellent), black tempera paint, easel brushes, water cups, white glue, newspapers.

Guidelines:

If you have solid connections with a lumber yard or even a cigar store this is the "in" activity for you. You may even find what the famous sculptress Louise Nevelson found in experimenting and arranging small scraps of wood within small spaces. This project also provides a good excuse to visit some nearby museum that has Nevelson sculpture on display and to enjoy comparing your own art to hers.

Variety and experimentation are the keys to success in creating a box sculpture. Varying the sizes and shapes of the small wood pieces is a must! Push your wood pieces around a bit and experiment with different arrangements. Some arrangements are more pleasing to the eyes than others. If you desire a more open type of sculpture, remove the top of the cigar box. This will permit you to work with taller pieces of wood, extending your sculpture even higher. It doesn't take much wood to create all the little pieces you need for the activity, but it does require a power saw of sorts and perhaps a friend to use it!

Try to resist the urge to completely fill the sculptural area with wood. Open spaces are as much a part of box sculpture as the wooden pieces are.

Box sculptures become more unified when painted a single color. Black, as Louise Nevelson uses, seems to create this visual impact. Try black tempera paint and start creating!

How to Do It:

1. Begin by collecting scrap wood pieces before the activity. Since most pieces of wood collected will be too large, make arrangements for cutting the wood into smaller pieces that will readily fit into the cigar box.

2. Organize the class into groups of four pupils each. Spread newspapers over tables or desks pushed together to protect the surface.

3. Begin the activity by placing various pieces of wood within the area of the cigar box. Experiment with different arrangements by moving these pieces around inside the box (Figure 6-L5-1).

4. Add more wood shapes until the bottom of the box is *almost* filled. Some open spaces should be left free. Use white glue to adhere the shapes to the bottom of the box. Wipe off any excess glue since water-based paints will resist the glue and leave bare spots (Figure 6-L5-2).

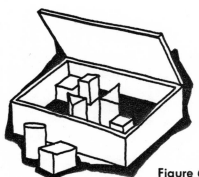

Figure 6-L5-1

Figure 6-L5-2

5. Distribute black tempera paint, water cups and easel brushes

Figure 6-L5-3

to each group. Paint the entire interior of the boxed sculpture (Figure 6-L5-3).

5. Paint the exterior of the box also.

7. Clean up by washing out brushes, water cups and throwing away scrap materials. Replace all caps on the tubes of glue. Save scrap wood for future activities.

Variations:

1. Use magazine pictures to create a montage on the cover of the box. Display the boxes someplace within the school.

2. Paint the tops of the wood pieces in different colors, adding visual impact.

LESSON 6

Start with a Broomstick!

Objectives:

1. To learn to work together on group art projects.

2. To learn to use various hand tools, work with various types of wood, and create large sculpture.

Materials:

Old broomsticks or a long piece of hard wood for use as a base, hammers, scrap wood of any kind, saws, hand drills, nails and wood screws, screwdrivers, white glue, black latex paint, 2-inch paint brushes, coffee cans, a bar of soap, newspapers.

Guidelines:

You don't have to be a witch to create your own broomstick sculpture, but you *do* need a long piece of wood and an additional stable piece of wood to use as a base. Working with large sculpture requires a few partners to share ideas and tasks, so begin picking some helpers you enjoy working with!

You'll need to collect a broomstick for each group sculpture. Pieces of pine will do the same job, but must be a minimum of two by two inches square. Most woods require pre-drilling holes before hammering in nails or twisting in screws. These pre-drilled holes prevent the wood from splitting. Another good trick is to rub every nail and screw in a bar of soap before inserting them into wood. At any rate, you need both nails and screws to hold all the wood pieces in your sculpture together.

Creating a large sculpture is definitely not a brief activity, so prepare for several hours of enjoyable work at drilling holes, hammering nails and inserting screws to create a permanent work of art for the foyer or hallway.

Even though those wood screws and nails look pretty firm in the wood, try adding white glue to each joint where wood meets to reinforce it. This added strength is necessary if you want to display your sculpture out in the halls where many hands will want to touch it. You may have to add weight to the wooden base if it begins to tip or tilt as the sculpture grows.

How to Do It:

1. Collect a variety of wood scraps including a five- or six-foot length of wood to use as an upright piece of the sculpture. In addition a two- or three-foot square piece of heavy plywood is necessary as a base for the upright piece.

2. Begin by drilling a hole through the plywood base and the bottom upright piece of wood. Use a long wood screw and white glue to fasten these two pieces together. Allow them to dry overnight before beginning work on the sculpture (Figure 6-L6-1).

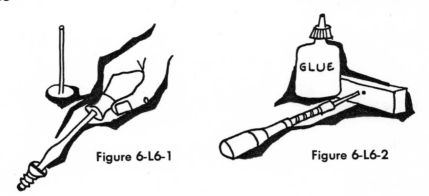

Figure 6-L6-1   Figure 6-L6-2

3. Add extensions of wood to the upright base piece. Pre-drill holes through these wood pieces before nailing or screwing them into position. Add glue where nails and screws are used to strengthen the joint (Figures 6-L6-2 and 3).

Figure 6-L6-3

4. Once the sculpture has been completely assembled, paint it, using black latex exterior house paint so that the art can be displayed outside. Make sure you use plenty of newspapers at this stage of the project and wear old shirts to protect clothing.

5. Clean the paint brushes, following directions on the can of latex paint. Throw away soiled newspapers and store scrap wood away in corrugated boxes.

Variations:

1. Hang objects on the sculpture to change its visual appearance.

2. Spray the entire sculpture with varnish and have it fastened to an exterior wall outside of the school.

LESSON 7

Flexible Shapes!

Objectives:

1. To learn to create colorful hanging sculpture from three-dimensional materials.

2. To develop a sensitivity and awareness to spaces and shapes in sculpture.

Materials:

Several pieces of 1/8″ × 1/8″-balsa strips, 36 inches long; stencil knives, Duco cement, common pins, colored cellophane, scissors, a large tray, water, large sheets of corrugated cardboard to work on; newspapers.

Guidelines:

Wood is generally a rigid material, giving way only to saws, gouges and mallets; the exception is balsa wood! Versatility is the one quality that makes balsa an easy and enjoyable material to work with. Add a little bit of water to soak the balsa and it becomes even more flexible, bending readily into almost any shape and held together with mere common pins!

It may not be necessary for you to soak your piece of balsa wood if the shape you create is a large one. Balsa will bend easily into most shapes, but be ready with a large tray and water in case you want to bend a piece of balsa into a tight curve. It will bend!

The number of shapes you can create from balsa may not be

endless but there is flexibility enough to create a great variety of shapes. Experiment with the balsa first, but be careful. Balsa will snap if you try to force it too far. See! Balsa *can* form circles, half circles, and football-like curved shapes that other non-flexible woods cannot.

Some of the shapes you experiment with may remind you of a subject. But you don't really need any specific theme to stimulate working with balsa. The material itself motivates you. Cutting, bending, pinning and gluing operations are all accomplished swiftly and easily. Now, how many materials can you make a statement like that about?

How to Do It:

1. Organize the class into small groups. Spread newspapers over tables to protect their surface. Pass out three 36-inch lengths of balsa, a stencil knife and several scraps of colored cellophane to each pupil. Each small group of pupils can share scissors, glue, pins and cement. A large tray filled with water should be placed on a nearby table.

2. Begin by experimenting with the balsa wood. Bend it, combine two pieces to see what different kinds of shapes you can create.

3. Once you have decided upon a basic shape, glue the pieces together and use pins pushed through both balsa pieces to hold the pieces in place until dry (Figure 6-L7-1).

4. Place other lengths of balsa across the basic shape and cut these with a stencil knife to fit tightly *within the shape*. Glue into position (Figure 6-L7-2).

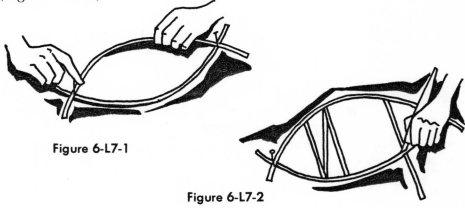

Figure 6-L7-1

Figure 6-L7-2

5. Continue to break up the space within the shape using more balsa strips. Vary the angles and locations of these additional pieces to create a variety of inner shapes.

6. Once all the additional pieces are in place, add additional cement to all the joints (Figure 6-L7-3).

7. Place scrap pieces of colored cellophane over *some of the inner shapes* created by the balsa strips. Use fast-drying cement (lightly) to adhere the cellophane to the balsa. Trim the excess cellophane with a sharp stencil knife (Figure 6-L7-4).

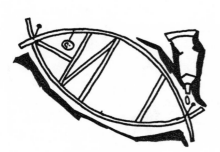

Figure 6-L7-3

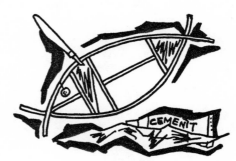

Figure 6-L7-4

8. Throw away small scraps. Replace tops on tubes of cement. Collect the pins in an envelope and wash up!

Variations:

1. Hang all of the completed cellophane-balsa sculpture in front of a window to create a mobile of individual pieces.

2. If cellophane is not available, use opaque colored papers to add color to the sculpture.

LESSON 8

Wood Photo Cubes!

Objectives:

1. To learn to use a combination of materials to create dimensional art.

2. To develop a sensitivity toward creating individualized themes or subjects.

Materials:

Old building blocks or pieces of 6-inch by 6-inch pine lumber cut into squares; magazine photographs or illustrations, rubber cement or gloss starch, old paint brushes, newspapers, scissors, one quart of shellac or a commercial decoupage liquid; alcohol for cleaning brushes (if shellac is used).

Guidelines:

Want to see everything from all sides objectively—even four sides of an issue? Then create your own photo cubes by starting with a block of wood and let your visual imagination go. You can stick vacation photographs or just beautiful "things" from a magazine on the wood cubes. At any rate, the "square" you create will provide a source of interest for you, and others, for years in the future.

What do you need? Not much! The basic cube can be created out of any solid material that is already square, cut to shape from wood or even created from cardboard. With a little gloss starch from the grocer's (omit the bluing), or rubber cement, you can adhere any magazine picture to the cube. Real photographs may require rubber cement instead of gloss starch, since they are slightly heavier in substance than magazine pictures.

Think of one theme or subject to develop: sports, people, Africa; almost any theme of individual interest can be carried out over all six sides of your cube. Use only five sides if you're short of pictures.

How to Do It:

1. Collect cubes at least six inches in diameter for each pupil. Begin saving magazines containing photographs and illustrations.

2. Distribute magazines, cubes, scissors, brushes, gloss starch or rubber cement to each small group of pupils. Shellac is used to seal the magazine photographs on the cube after they are dry, usually the following day.

3. Cut photographs, illustrations, or any appealing subject from old magazines. Try to develop a single theme (Figure 6-L8-1).

4. Use the largest photographs first in order to cover more space on the cube. Trim these photos to fit the cube (Figure 6-L8-2).

Figure 6-L8-1   Figure 6-L8-2

Apply gloss starch, or rubber cement, to one side of the cube at a time, adhering the trimmed photographs or designs to the starched surface. Sometimes a sharp blade is necessary to cut through bubbles that form. Press these flat (Figure 6-L8-3).

6. Use a commercial decoupage liquid, or shellac, to seal or "antique" the newly covered surfaces of the cube. One side of the cube should be left uncovered. Allow time for the cube to dry (Figure 6-L8-4).

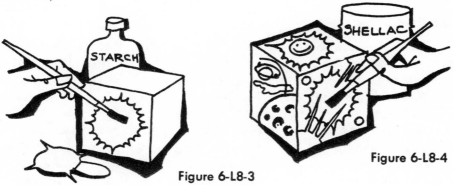

Figure 6-L8-3

Figure 6-L8-4

7. Clean up all paper scraps and soak shellac brushes in alcohol thoroughly. If gloss starch was used, wash those brushes in soapy water as soon as possible. Throw away all scraps with shellac odor *outdoors*. Burn the scraps.

Variations:

1. Use small cardboard boxes instead of wood or plastic and paint a zodiac sign on each side. Use this theme to develop interest in astronomy.

Alphabet-Wood Jewelry

Objectives:

    1. To learn to combine different materials to create jewelry.

    2. To develop the ability to arrange objects into designs.

Materials:

Tongue depressors or small wood scraps, white glue, rickrack, paper doilies, napkins, buttons and other small found objects; bar pins, packages of dried alphabet soup, scissors, stain and varnish, old brushes (optional), small saws for light wood, newspapers.

Guidelines:

Would you like to see your name in print? Run to your local grocery store and purchase some dried alphabet soup noodles. With these letters and a few other found materials you'll be ready to create your own truly individualized jewelry or make a very personal thing for your closest friend or relative.

Tongue depressors are the most common material available in schools, and also the easiest to use as a base for your original jewelry. The wood of tongue depressors can be sawed easily into various shapes, stained, varnished, and even glued easily. After you've found all the tongue depressors you need to work with, start searching for small objects to add to the design. The more materials the better the jewelry will be. Search carefully for small rickrack, or braided edging, small pearl buttons, paper doilies, and any other small shiny objects that will add luster to your jewelry.

If you prefer simplicity, merely stain the tongue depressors, using a brush, add a coat of shellac and wait a day before gluing your alphabet soup letters to the finished wood surface.

White glue is the only adhesive you will need to adhere materials to your pin. Since this type of glue is slow drying, a little patience is required—as well as a little pressure to help stick objects together.

172

How to Do It:

1. Saw tongue depressors into various designed shapes, using a small saw, as an activity prior to the actual lesson (Figure 6-L9-1).

Figure 6-L9-1

2. Organize the class into groups and distribute tongue depressors, white glue, alphabet soup letters, scissors, bar pins, and several types of found materials to each group. Cover desks with newspapers.

3. Use white glue to cover the tongue depressor with found materials as a background for the jewelry (Figure 6-L9-2).

4. Arrange alphabet soup letters and other found objects to the background. Use white glue to adhere into place (Figure 6-L9-3).

5. Allow the pin to dry overnight. Turn the pin over and use white glue to adhere to bar pin to the reverse side of the jewelry (Figure 6-L9-4).

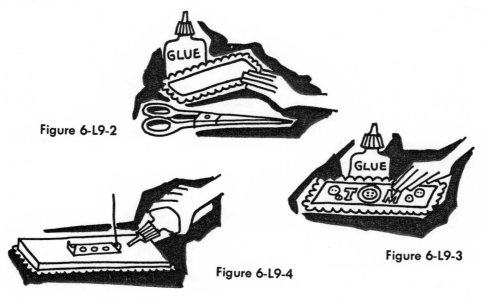

Figure 6-L9-2

Figure 6-L9-3

Figure 6-L9-4

6. Clean up by throwing away all small scraps. Wipe any excess white glue from desk surfaces and throw away newspapers that are not usable. Replace all tools and materials to their proper locations and wash up.

Variations:

1. Stain the tongue depressors with wood stain and clear shellac as a background for the alphabet soup letters.

2. Paint the tongue depressor with latex paint and create a short saying, instead of a name, on the pin.

CHAPTER 7

Using Cloth and Clay

INTRODUCTION TO CLOTH AND CLAY

Most children have few art experiences using either cloth or clay materials before they reach school age. Because of this factor, these materials should be explored simply, with few product goals, until the children gain security and knowledge. Creative expectations and high standards need to be set aside temporarily, until pupils fully explore the possibilities of the materials.

Creating with a pliable material, such as cloth, may be a simple activity for some pupils but can present problems to others. Pupils who draw well may find experimenting with cloth difficult because they react more readily to realism and visualization than arranging materials into designs. Observe individual pupil differences closely during the activity to assess individual pupil strengths and weaknesses for future lessons. You'll find some pupils highly successful using three-dimensional materials, but not as successful in drawing or painting, and vice versa.

Cloth is a very versatile art medium, usually used in combination with other related materials such as: yarn, thread, felt, string and rug pieces in weaving, collage, stitchery and applique.

Clay is a basic art medium for all age levels. Several different types of clay are practical for use in contemporary elementary school programs. These are: Plasticine, a permanent type of soft oil base clay; ceramic clay, for firing permanently in a high temperature kiln; and self-hardening clay, a semi-permanent type of clay that hardens at room temperature, or in low temperature kilns.

Clay is an excellent introduction to three-dimensional art for young children and can be used in combination with other art materials to extend the possibilities of the medium.

Cloth and Clay Materials

Activities using cloth are limited in scope unless large quantities of material are collected long before activities are ready to begin. Start by saving old pillowcases, sheets and pieces of muslin in addition to a variety of nylon, wool, acrylic and cotton cloth. Even scrap rug materials add different textures to collages that cannot be duplicated by any other material.

Once pupils in your class become aware that cloth is a functional art medium, they will become the most important source for finding new materials. Do not, however, overlook local rug or decorating centers, which are excellent sources for scrap materials.

Clay activities must be planned well ahead of time. Until it is used, clay should be stored in dark, cool, moist locations. Ceramic clays that are fired in a kiln (often pronounced "kill") must be wedged; this means thrown continuously on a hard surface until compactly compressed. Wedging eliminates the air bubbles in the clay that might expand and burst when fired at high temperatures.

Color may be added to clay several different ways; the most common method is painting fired clay with ceramic glazes and refiring in a kiln. Most dried clay surfaces can be sprayed with enamel paints. Self-hardening clay can be painted by brush with any type of opaque paint and varnished to protect the surface.

Organizing for Cloth and Clay Activities

Cloth and clay activities are best organized into small groups of four to six pupils in order to share the necessary materials and tools. Individual desks can be moved together to create larger working surfaces if classrooms lack tables.

Tools and supplies basic to most cloth activities include: small- and large-eyed needles, embroidery floss, yarn, colored burlap, felt, muslin or white cotton cloth, cold water dyes and glues suitable for fabrics. Cloth scraps brought to school by students may be shared by all to expand the variety of materials available to each pupil.

Clay requires a damp-proof base to protect working surfaces from its moisture. Oilcloth, cut into yard square pieces, is the best material available. Use the rough, unpolished surface of the oilcloth to avoid "sticking" clay. If oilcloth is not readily available, one-inch thick pads of newspapers may be substituted. Newspaper will withstand excess moisture for the length of time necessary to complete any clay activities.

Basic tools, supplies and equipment necessary for working with ceramic firing clay include: small wooden tools to create details, oilcloth, wire to cut through clay, and high-firing glazes. Other tools are desirable but are not required to complete simple clay activities. Fingers and hands are the best "tools" to shape clay.

Common Problems in Cloth and Clay Activities

Both cloth and clay activities require the development of some skills. These skills and experiences are gained through beginning with several simple, exploratory activities before progressing to more complex activities. If basic experiences are not provided, students will encounter a great variety of problems in using the materials.

There are several common problems pupils usually encounter when first learning to manipulate clay. These are: (1) children tend to work too thinly with clay, pinching out delicate appendages; encourage these pupils to roll clay to quarter-inch thicknesses and pinch out thick tails or legs from their main clay body; (2) any solid clay art work must be hollowed out internally or it may explode during the firing process; (3) pupils must learn to add moisture continuously to drying clay that begins to show fine line cracks; this is accomplished by dipping one finger into water and adding the moisture to the drying clay surface; (4) if clay pieces break in the kiln it may mean that (a) they were poorly wedged or modeled; (b) too solid and not hollowed out; (c) fired without being thoroughly dried; (d) fired too quickly at high temperatures without permitting moisture release from the kiln.

Working with cloth poses some problems for elementary age pupils. They must learn to thread needles, tie knots, cut fabric and plan their activities before using the materials. All of these activities are not natural experiences that all children ordinarily use, or are familiar with. They must be demonstrated and taught.

Cutting soft materials, such as felt or wool, requires more skill than cutting through firm materials, such as paper. If pupils have problems cutting paper, these cutting problems will be exaggerated with cloth. There may be several reasons why pupils cut poorly. The scissors may be dull, pupils may be cutting with the points instead of the back edge of the scissor blades, or pupils may not be holding the scissors at a right angle to the material. Check these points carefully if your class has problems with cutting.

Some cloth activities, such as collage, require gluing two pieces of cloth together. Usually white glue or rubber cement will perform this adhering adequately. Glue requires some time to really dry and set, however, so cloth pieces should not be handled too roughly until they do dry out.

Stitchery presents unusual design problems for most pupils, since they tend to work with line rather than solid areas. This may be compensated for by combining solid felt shapes to line stitchery designs.

USING CLOTH AND CLAY

CLOTH OR CLAY ACTIVITY (GRADE LEVEL)	NEW MATERIALS INTRODUCED	PHYSICAL SKILLS INVOLVED	PUPILS LEARN	EMOTIONAL AND INTELLECTUAL EXPERIENCES
Putting Pieces Together (Collage) (3-6)	Corrugated cardboard Found materials	Assembling pieces. Gluing. Cutting a variety of materials.	To use a combination of materials. To use the principle of overlapping to create design.	Arranging Selecting Deciding Exploring Combining
Dyeing for Color (Tie Dyeing) (3-6)	Cold-water dye	Using elastic bands. Handling wet materials.	The process of dyeing cloth to create designs.	Selecting Experimenting Trying Out
Hold It Up High (Felt Banners) (5-6)	Colored felt	Cutting through soft material. Gluing felt.	To create original cut patterns. To emphasize color contrast in design.	Visualizing Designing Elaborating Comparing
Wax and Dye (Wax Crayon Batik) (3-6)	Cold-water dye	Handling wet material. Drawing on cloth with wax crayons.	To use new combinations of materials.	Visualizing Discovering Detailing
Making Clay Pictures (3-6)	Self-hardening clay Metallic spray paint	Modeling clay Texturing clay Spraying paint	The fundamentals of designing. To arrange and compare parts of a composition.	Arranging Deciding Composing Designing
Imaginary Animals (Clay Sculpture) (2-6)	Self-hardening clay Texture tools	Modeling pliable material. Creating small details. Assembling parts.	To fasten pieces of clay together. To create textural surfaces. To sculpt three dimensionally.	Imagining Inventing Exploring Ideas Origination Synthesizing
Lifting the Edges (Slab Clay Surfaces) (3-6)	Rolling pins Texture tools	Rolling out clay. Cutting clay. Imprinting a surface using tools.	To create free-form sculptural shapes. To emphasize textural surfaces.	Creating Exploring Elaborating
Something to Wear (Ceramic-Enamel Jewelry) (5-6)	Enamels combined with clay	Shaping and texturing small pieces. Handling small tools. Sifting powder.	To use a combination of new materials. To create small designs and textures.	Creating Composing Exploring Materials
Make an Impression (Casting Plaster into Clay) (4-6)	Plaster of Paris	Pouring plaster. Incising, wedging and drawing on clay.	To create a cast impression. To work with a variety of materials.	Reproducing Original Ideas Visualizing

Putting Pieces Together

Objectives:

1. To learn to arrange and compose using a variety of found materials.

2. To learn the process of visual synthesis.

Materials:

Scrap cloth of various sizes and textures, colored corrugated paper, brown corrugated cardboard (background), scissors, school paste, white glue, small pieces of found objects such as buttons, hardware, feathers, etc., newspapers.

Guidelines:

A collage is a piece of art formed by fastening a variety of materials onto a flat surface. There is always a bit of excitement before the collage is assembled, as you begin thinking about how to use the materials you have collected. With a few pieces of large corrugated cardboard and several different pieces of cloth and metal, a great design may be born!

Spend some time collecting a variety of materials before beginning your collage. This time may be the most important phase in creating a successful collage. Collecting materials also provides ample time for you to incubate ideas, backgrounds, textures and all the thinking involved in creating a collage.

Search your garage for little pieces of shiny metal, old springs, or any other small hardware pieces that look interesting. Search the attic for out-dated, velvet pieces, or richly-patterned material your grandmother left you. These discards will provide material and color for the large, irregular, overlapping shapes making up the background of your collage. Large corrugated boxes will provide the strong background on which to adhere all the different materials. Thinner cardboard materials tend to curl and warp under the weight of collage materials and drying glues.

179

Once you've gathered all the materials that you need, start the collage by adhering large overlapping shapes of different materials on a pre-cut corrugated background. Sheets of thin, colored corrugated paper can be torn into various shapes and added to the design. A knife or large scissors may be needed to cut old rugs. Experiment by overlapping your shapes and materials in various ways on the corrugated cardboard. Rearrange these shapes until you are pleased with the composition and then glue them firmly into position.

After the background begins to shape up, start exploring where to place your three-dimensional materials. Notice how well those seagull feathers you saved last summer go with that old broken strand of costume pearls? Glue them right into place! Add small touches to your collage with small pieces of metal hardware. Allow lots of time for the white glue to "set" before handling the collage.

How to Do It:

1. Collect a variety of collage materials prior to beginning the activity. Store them in boxes until beginning the activity. Pre-cut a piece of corrugated cardboard to size for each collage, the larger the better!

2. Cover desks with newspaper prior to the activity and distribute all materials to groups of pupils.

3. Cut and tear a variety of large shapes from different background materials (Figures 7-L1-1 and 2).

Figure 7-L1-1

Figure 7-L1-2

4. Overlap these background shapes on a corrugated cardboard background. Use white glue or paste to adhere the shapes into final position (Figure 7-L1-3).

5. Experiment placing smaller materials and textures overlapping the background shapes. Use white glue or school paste to adhere the materials permanently (Figure 7-L1-4).

6. Carefully carry the completed collage to an isolated drying area protected by newspapers.

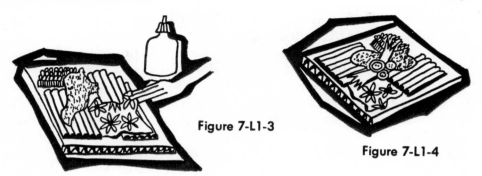

Figure 7-L1-3

Figure 7-L1-4

7. Clean up by storing the scrap cloth materials for future activities, removing white glue spots with a damp cloth and throwing away protective newspapers. Wash up!

Variations:

1. Create miniature collages using tiny materials.

2. Work together as a group to create one large collage for a hallway bulletin board or on a large piece of fiberboard or plywood.

LESSON 2

Dyeing for Color!

Objectives:

1. To learn to use cold-water dyes to design on cloth.

2. To learn to experiment, using a variety of materials.

Materials:

Large pieces of white cotton or muslin cloth, cold-water dyes, large plastic buckets, pails of water, string or small elastic bands, yardsticks or rulers, newspapers.

Guidelines:

Being tied into knots can be fun, if you are the lucky piece of cloth about to be initiated into the ancient art of dyeing. Relax, you're going to enjoy mixing dyes and tying cloth to create designs on old tee shirts or sections of discarded bed sheets. Besides, there's quite a bit of history connected to the art of dyeing that will provide interesting information for a study of different cultures.

A few old bed sheets will provide material for everyone to experiment with the process of dyeing. Not all cloth material can be easily dyed; some polyesters and acrylics do not absorb dyes as well as other cloth, and cotton absorbs dye very quickly. Test all the materials involved before beginning this activity; there are differences in the quality of household dyes and cloth that are unpredictable. Read the directions on the package of dye carefully to be certain that you are purchasing the right dye for your specific cloth. Cold-water dyes that do not require boiling water to dissolve are easier to use with large groups of pupils, but most hot water dyes provide brighter colors.

Spread lots of newspapers over your working surface. When your completed tie dye comes out of the pail, it will be dripping wet. What you do at this time with your damp design depends upon the directions found in your package of dye. Some dyed materials require rinsing with clear cold water, others need to "set" in liquid solutions, or are rolled in absorbent towels to dry. Read directions carefully before you begin dyeing.

You may actually tie your designs with string, but purchasing a package of tiny elastic bands makes tie dyeing a lot easier for children who have difficulty tying knots. A great variety of designs are possible, so give some thought as to which design you desire to create. Perhaps a rosette, sunburst, or irregular colored stripes appeal to you. Take your pick! The material that you are going to dye must be dampened first before you tie or fasten sections of the material with string or elastic bands. An old ruler should be used to submerge your design under the surface of the prepared dye, and also to lift the damp cloth out of the pail.

Be sure to wear old clothes on the day you set aside to tie dye!

How to Do It:

1. Wash and pre-cut the clean white cotton cloth, or muslin, into pieces. A 16- to 20-inch square piece of material is adequate for first attempts (Figure 7-L2-1).

2. Mix the cold-water dye in large plastic pails, according to directions on the package. Spread newspapers over a working surface located near the drying area. Distribute the materials each pupil needs:

Figure 7-L2-1   **Figure 7-L2-2**

water to dampen cloth, elastic bands or string, pads of newspapers to protect each desk (Figure 7-L2-2).

3. Show samples of various tie-dye designs and demonstrate how they were tied or fastened to create each design. (Figure 7-L2-3).

4. Immerse the cloth under clear water to dampen it and "tie" a selected design using string or small elastic bands.

Figure 7-L2-3

Figure 7-L2-4

5. Carry the completed tie dye on a pad of newspapers to the table prepared for dyeing. Use a ruler to immerse the design under the surface. Remove the soaked design, following recommended times for the particular brand of dye color (Figure 7-L2-4).

6. Place the wet design on a pad of newspapers and carry it to a drying area (or to another soaking area to set the color if package directions require this additional step).

7. Throw away old newspapers, and wash hands carefully with soap and water. Pour excess dye colors down custodial sinks and run water through the sink. Save excess cloth for future activities.

Variations:

1. Follow up initial dyeing activities with more complex projects, such as dyeing tee shirts, or larger surfaces.

2. Create your own dye colors from organic materials found in nature. Formulas for natural dyes can be found in books and magazine articles about weaving or spinning fabrics.

LESSON 3

Hold It Up High!

Objectives:

1. To learn to create complex and elaborate designs.
2. To learn to create heraldry designs, using colored felt.

Materials:

Colored felt, scissors, 18 × 24-inch manila paper or newsprint, black crayons, pins, white glue, paper towels, newspapers.

Guidelines:

Everyone is entitled to create his own emblazoned felt banner and hold it up high, or perhaps mount it on the wall for all to admire! Although felt is a soft and luxurious material to work with, it has some limitations. However, these limitations are more than compensated for by the fact that creating individual banners readily lends itself to learning about heraldry, knighthood and medieval lore. An interesting topic!

Begin by studying heraldry and the coats-of-arms of your own family ancestors. Note carefully the symbols that artists of old used to draw to create visual statements about the deeds and characteristics of a particular family heritage. Perhaps your family's coat-of-arms pictures a deer or a wild boar, proclaiming their skill in hunting. Think about the challenges of creating your own original heraldry design! What skills would you symbolize? What deeds should be honored?

If you lack experience cutting felt, practice your cutting skills on a few simple designs first before creating large banners. You'll find that felt is easily cut by using the lower part of the scissors' blades rather than the points. Hold the scissors at a 90-degree angle when cutting felt to gain full effectiveness of the scissors' edge. Most poor cutters ignore this simple rule.

Sketch your heraldry ideas on scrap paper first. Beginning without thinking about ideas is a sure path to lower standards! Once your idea is well-conceived, draw it to scale on paper the exact size of your banner. The larger the better! What colors seem appropriate to your design? Better indicate colors and shapes on your design to help guide you later on. Once your design is fully drawn to scale, cut the drawing apart to create paper patterns that can be pinned to the correct felt colors and cut out. Some thinking about which pieces of felt need to be cut first and adhered to the background color is necessary.

Most white glues are functional for adhering felt to felt. Keep your fingers clean by wiping off excess glue on paper towels. Once the glue has dried, it must be peeled from the fingers!

How to Do It:

After motivating the class about heraldry:

1. Distribute all materials to individual pupils after each desk has been protected by several sheets of newspapers.

2. Use a black crayon to sketch out ideas on a small piece of paper. Select the best design and draw it on paper the same size as the final felt banner (Figure 7-L3-1).

3. Select a basic, colored felt background that will contrast well with the other colors in the design and cut it to the desired shape (Figure 7-L3-2).

Figure 7-L3-1

Figure 7-L3-2

4. Indicate the colors to be used in the design by writing them on the drawing, or coloring the design.

5. Cut out the first large shapes of the pattern from the drawing.

6. Pin each paper shape onto the proper piece of colored felt and cut around the paper pattern (Figure 7-L3-3).

7. Use white glue to adhere each cut shape to the basic background color (Figure 7-L3-4).

Figure 7-L3-3

Figure 7-L3-4

8. Continue to cut and adhere smaller details to the banner until it is completed. Mount the finalized heraldry design on a piece of dowel or an old broomstick (Figure 7-L3-5).

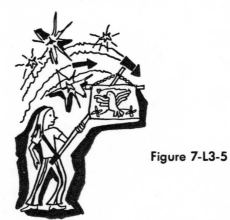

Figure 7-L3-5

9. Clean up by saving large scraps of felt, collecting tools and throwing away scrap material. Peel dried white glue from fingers before washing up with soap.

Variations:

1. If ample felt material is not readily available for large banners, work in miniature, using smaller amounts of material.

2. Work as a total group to create one, or several, large banners that represent the ideas of many individuals.

LESSON 4

Wax and Dye!

Objectives:

1. To learn to use cold-water dyes.
2. To learn about the batik process.

Materials:

Crayons, white cotton handkerchiefs (or old pillowcases), cold-water dyes, an electric iron, large coffee cans, rolls of paper toweling, a large wooden spoon, newspapers.

Guidelines:

Need a bright new scarf, an ascot, or perhaps a colorful wall hanging for your room? Batik wax-resist dyeing is the answer. You don't have to become a batik expert who patiently sits by a lamp with his "tjanting" needle. A few pieces of colored crayons and cold-water dyes are all you need to create a design that will "pass" as a real batik.

Read the directions on the packages of dyes before you purchase any. Some dyes require boiling, others may function only for silk or acetate cloth. You need to know which type of cloth you are dyeing and purchase the correct dye for it. Cold-water dyes are seldom as brilliant or intense in color as dyes that simmer over a hot plate, so play safe and test the strength of your dyes first. You may want to use less water than the directions on the package call for. This will increase the intensity of the color considerably.

Dyeing can be neat, or it can be messy. Look around for an old shirt if you are going to be the person who does all the dipping into the dye pot. Spread a lot of newspapers and paper toweling underneath the drying cloth. Don't leave too much distance between the pots of cold-water dye and the drying area or you'll soon be scrubbing up a multitude of spots from the floor.

What shall we design? An elephant? Flowers? Think about it and discuss which subjects may lend themselves to batik. It may be all right to draw a zodiac sign on a scarf for a friend, but if you want an apt gift for mother, flowers may be more appropriate.

After the design has dried overnight, the wax crayon may be "set" using an electric iron and newspaper to protect the batik design.

How to Do It:

1. Distribute crayons, pre-cut white cloth and a half-inch pad of newspapers to each pupil. Establish an area for drying the completed batik close to large pails on a table well protected with newspapers. Select one or two pupils to mix dyes and handle all the wet material, although each pupil should dye his own batik (Figure 7-L4-1).

2. Use a crayon to draw a design directly on the cloth. Press rather hard on the crayon or trace over the crayon lines a second time (Figure 7-L4-2).

Figure 7-L4-2

Figure 7-L4-1

3. Carry the completed wax design to the dyeing table. Immerse the cloth into the dye water, pushing it under the surface with a large wooden spoon. Repeat this process until the cloth is impregnated with color (Figure 7-L4-3).

Figure 7-L4-3

4. Remove the damp cloth from the water, stretching it out on a paper towel over a pad of newspapers. Carry this to the drying area.

5. The damp material will dry overnight. The wax crayon color must be "set" into the cloth by heat. Place the batik design on a pad of newspapers, using a single sheet of newspaper to cover the design. Use a heated electric iron to "set" the crayon design permanently (Figure 7-L4-4).

Figure 7-L4-4

6. Clean up all damp newspapers, pour the colored dyes into the soil outside the school. Save the wooden spoon and check for any spots on the floor. Wash up!

Variations:

1. Organize the class into groups and have each group create a mural using the batik process.

2. Repeat the activity, using heated dye colors. With experience, the second activity should improve greatly.

LESSON 5

Making Clay Pictures

Objectives:

1. To learn to create textures in clay surfaces.

2. To learn the art of bas-relief and sculpting in the "half-round."

Materials:

Self-hardening clay, corrugated cardboard pieces approximately 12 × 16 inches, large scissors or a paper cutter, two 16-ounce cans of gold, metallic spray paint, large cardboard box, newspapers or oilcloth, odorless turpentine, old rags.

Guidelines:

First experiences with clay usually lead you through many mazes. But once that first introductory experience with clay has been successfully completed, you are ready to add to your knowledge about clay and how to texture its surface. Changing the surface of soft ceramic clay and creating a variety of textures initiates the novice artist to surface design.

Bas-relief, a generally flat surface with half-rounded figures, is an ancient sculptural art form. You'll find that Assyrians, Egyptians and Romans practiced sculpture in the half round as decoration for their architecture. Creating bas-relief designs provides a good opportunity to correlate art with history.

You'll find some subjects for your bas-relief picture are easier to create than others. Try your hand at landscapes with trees and animals, circuses or under-water scenes. The key to good relief design is found in not completely filling the background area, leaving much of the background free. Think of each object in your clay picture as a separate and isolated design (see illustrations).

You'll find that clay readily adheres to corrugated cardboard. Create your picture completely before thinking about texturing the clay surface. Textures in clay can be created without using tools. Fingers, when coordinated with a little thought, can create almost any type of texture. And, besides, it's more fun to really "get into the clay."

Spraying your final masterpiece is easy, but be careful! It is usually best to spray the relief design outdoors but if you must spray indoors, try spraying within the confines of a large box. Since the person spraying is bound to get paint on his hands, try limiting this task to one or two individuals, who should wear old shirts. Spray paint won't travel far indoors, but handling the painted objects will cause some paint smears. Gold spray paint adds a certain richness to the final clay picture that cannot be matched by other spray colors. Open classroom windows whenever you paint or use turpentine!

You'll be happy with your final bas-relief. Why not display the masterpiece so that others will become interested in this simple, but effective, clay activity?

How to Do It:

1. Use large scissors to pre-cut pieces of corrugated cardboard to approximately 12 × 16 inches, or 9 × 12 inches for younger pupils (Figure 7-L5-1).

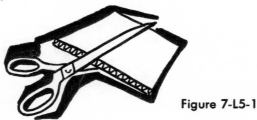

Figure 7-L5-1

2. Cover each pupil's desk with one-inch thick pads of newspapers. Establish a spraying area covered with newspapers, with a large box to spray into. Lay other protective newspapers in an isolated area for drying purposes.

3. Distribute a large handful of ceramic clay to each pupil.

4. Press the clay onto the corrugated cardboard surface to create an upraised picture. Leave open areas in the composition (Figure 7-L5-2).

5. Once the clay picture has been completed, add various textures to the clay surfaces using your fingers (Figure 7-L5-3).

Figure 7-L5-2

Figure 7-L5-3

6. Carry the completed clay picture, on its pad of newspapers, to the spraying area. Make certain some windows are open to reduce odor.

7. Place the clay design, still on the newspaper pad, in a large box. Spray the picture lightly with gold enamel paint until the clay and cardboard surfaces are covered (Figure 7-L5-4).

Figure 7-L5-4

8. Carry the wet design on its newspaper pad to a drying area covered with newspapers.

9. Clean up by using turpentine on a rag cloth to remove any paint spots. Crumple and throw away old newspapers, boxes and cardboard. Replace good clay in its tightly-covered container. Everyone should wash up using hot water and soap after handling painted materials.

Variations:

1. Use metallic spray paint to decorate other, fully round, clay designs.

LESSON 6

Imaginary Animals

Objectives:

1. To learn to use imagination in the creation of original clay sculpture.

2. To learn to use self-hardening, or plasticine, clay emphasizing textural surfaces.

Materials:

Oil-based plasticine clay or non-firing, self-hardening clay; pencils, or boxwood tools; water cups, oilcloth or pads of newspapers.

Guidelines:

Exercise your imagination daily and it will expand as surely as trained muscles. If you haven't been exercising mentally lately, why not begin right now by thinking about creating an imaginary clay animal?

Have your imaginative ideas become rigid through lack of use? Loosen them by thinking about any two unusually different animals and how they might be combined together to create one entirely new imaginary animal. How about combining an eagle and an alligator? You can rename your animal an "eagator" or an "alligle." Unusual characteristics, such as thin legs and long necks may be tempting targets, but remember that self-hardening clay may not bear the weight of these extended appendages. Oil-based plasticine-type clay is a bit firmer and will support most animal sculpture.

You'll find that your imaginary animal will be greatly improved by adding surface textures to the completed form, using small tools to texture the clay. These changes in the clay surface create textural contrasts within your sculpture, adding those little "differences" that result in better art.

Anything from pencils to small pieces of metal hardware can be used to imprint textures into plasticine clay. Start exploring the kitchen and garage for the small objects you'll need to create textures.

When creating with oil-based clay, it is not necessary to smoothen the clay surface, as it is when using self-hardening clay. Self-hardening clay can be smoothed by dipping one finger into water and rubbing the clay surface. This smoothing is always done before adding textures to the clay.

How to Do It:

After discussing combining two different kinds of animals:

1. Cover the desks with thick pads of newspapers or the reverse side of shiny oilcloth.

2. Distribute full, double handfuls of self-hardening clay, or one-pound slabs of softened oil-based clay to each pupil (Figure 7-L6-1).

Figure 7-L6-1

3. Distribute small objects or tools for texturing the clay surface. Fill water cups if self-hardening clay is used.

4. Create the basic body shape of your combined imaginary animals. If oil-based clay is used, it must be pre-softened near heat, or by pressing firmly with hands. If self-hardening clay is used, continuously add moisture to the clay by dipping fingers in water (Figure 7-L6-2).

5. Clay appendages such as legs, necks, heads or wings are formed and added to the body, using a pencil to roughen both clay surfaces before joining them firmly together. This creates stronger clay joints (Figure 7-L6-3).

Figure 7-L6-2

Figure 7-L6-3

6. Use a variety of small objects to create textural details in the clay surface (Figure 7-L6-4).

Figure 7-L6-4

7. Store self-hardening clay pieces away from heat sources to dry. Self-hardening clay may be sprayed with enamel paint or varnish to decorate and protect its surface (Figure 7-L6-5).

8. Clean up by throwing away small scraps and newspapers.

Figure 7-L6-5

Oilcloth may be washed in the sink and small tools set to soak. Wash hands with soap and water!

Variations:

1. Combine a group of imaginary animal sculptures in a diorama, adding natural materials and a background.

2. Follow up imaginary animal sculpture by writing creative stories about the animals.

LESSON 7

Lifting the Edges

Objectives:

1. To learn to create functional clay objects.

2. To develop experiences utilizing clay skills and learn to emphasize form and texture in three-dimensional design.

Materials:

Ceramic firing clay, small tools or objects for texturing clay; old dinner knives, large pieces of oilcloth or pads of newspapers, 12-inch strips of 1/4-inch thick wood or thick rulers, rolling pins, watercolor cups, pencil, a ceramic kiln.

Guidelines:

Clay can be a very deceiving medium because it is so manipulative and easy to sculpt into three-dimensional shapes. True enough! But clay is so easy to use that sometimes the final results end up as unimaginative clay snakes or traditional little rabbits. Why not strive for a more functional use of clay and still keep the gates of creativity open? This openness can be accomplished through thinking about objects that will be useful at home. Something for the bathroom, as a soap-holder? A shallow pot to hold cactus, or a long dish to contain food?

Begin by selecting a double handful of ceramic firing clay and flattening it somewhat on a piece of oilcloth, using the rough side. The clay is flattened further by using rolling pins to reduce its thickness between two pieces of wood or thick rulers. These wood strips also help to control an even thickness of the clay. Use a pencil to draw a large free-form shape into the clay surface. This shape will provide the foundation for learning about a variety of textures.

Use an old dinner knife to cut completely around your clay shape and remove it from the rolled-out clay. Smooth the clay surface, using one finger dipped in water.

Now is the time to think about texture! Use small objects to imprint textures into the damp clay surface before you begin lifting the edges of your clay shape.

Roll several different sizes of clay balls, lift the edges of your clay shape from its flat base, using the clay balls to support the upraised free-form shape and add dimension. Allow the piece to dry thoroughly with the supporting clay pieces still in position. The dried clay should feel like cool leather when placed against your cheek.

How to Do It:

1. Distribute pads of newspapers to protect each desk surface, and watercolor cups to each group of pupils. Direct pupils to select their own clay. A large handful of clay should be sufficient for the project. Distribute sticks, texture tools and all other materials to groups of pupils at tables.

2. Use the palms of your hands to flatten the clay on a piece of reversed oilcloth.

3. Place two spacing sticks a distance apart, so that a rolling pin may be used to equalize the thickness of the clay. Roll out the clay between the two sticks (Figure 7-L7-1).

Figure 7-L7-1

4. Use a pencil to draw a free-form shape in the surface of the rolled clay. Cut excess clay away from the drawn shape with a dinner knife (Figure 7-L7-2).

5. Smooth the surface of the clay shape, using a finger dipped in water.

6. Imprint texture in the clay, using a variety of small tools and objects (Figure 7-L7-3).

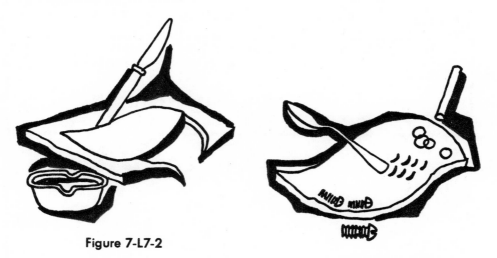

Figure 7-L7-2

Figure 7-L7-3

7. Roll small balls of clay of different sizes. Lift the edges of the clay shape and use the clay balls to support the raised clay edges (Figure 7-L7-4).

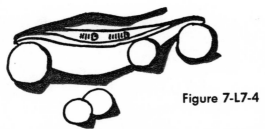

Figure 7-L7-4

8. Store the clay away from heat and allow to dry until each piece feels like leather when applied to your cheek (approximately two to three days).

9. Fire the clay pieces in a ceramic kiln at 1800°.

10. Throw away excess scrap materials, soak texturing tools, rulers, and water cups. Wash up with soap and water!

Variations:

1. Use the same textural techniques on flat clay surfaces to create many tiles that can be used for a ceramic mural cemented to a wall surface.

2. Follow up by glazing each piece and refiring.

LESSON 8

Something to Wear

Objectives:

1. To learn to design simple original jewelry.

2. To learn to synthesize a variety of art media into new combinations.

Materials:

Ceramic firing clay, mini-objects to create textures in the clay; powdered enamels, lollipop sticks, pencil, water cups, cord or necklace chain (optional); a ceramic kiln, newspapers.

Guidelines:

Looking for something original to hang around your neck or perhaps store away for a favorite birthday? Enameled ceramic jewelry may be just the simple answer you have been seeking. This combination of enamel and clay is exciting and easy to master, particularly if a small ceramic kiln is available to complete the firing process. Enamels add just the right touch of glossy color to clay. Clay is easy to form into shapes and simple to texture. These two major characteristics of the materials combine to provide immediate results.

You'll need either a small ceramic kiln, or a sophisticated three-heat, electric enameling kiln, to control the slow, upward movement of heat required to fire a combination of clay and enamels. Enamels can withstand the quick rising temperature of an enameling kiln, but clay cannot.

Explore several different jewelry shapes by drawing into the surface of flattened clay with a pointed stick or pencil. Once you've found just the right shape for your particular jewelry, incise all the way through the clay and cut it out. Smooth the rough edges of the clay shape with your wet finger.

Start thinking about textures. Look around the room for small tools or objects that you can use to indent the clay surface. These tools must be fairly small since your jewelry is usually rather limited in size. Think small! If you're creating a necklace, use a lollipop stick to punch a hole in the clay for the chain or cord. Powdered enamels may be sprinkled directly on the wet clay surface with your fingers. Not too thickly! Enamels will melt and flow in the firing process as the clay dries. Fire the piece at 1450-1500 degrees (Cone 014), bringing the heat up very slowly.

Allow ample time for the clay jewelry to dry, away from heat sources, before firing it. Small pieces of clay will dry in a day. Don't fire the clay too quickly. Once the surface of the powdered enamels is visibly melted and shiny, turn off the electric kiln and let the jewelry cool slowly overnight. If you've never fired clay or enamels, ask for help from someone who has.

How to Do It:

1. Prepare the class for a clay activity by distributing all the tools and materials to pupils organized into small groups.

2. Cover tables with pads of newspapers.

3. Use the palm of your hand to flatten a small piece of ceramic

clay on a pad of newspapers. Use a pencil or pointed lollipop stick to draw a free-form shape into the clay surface (Figure 7-L8-1).

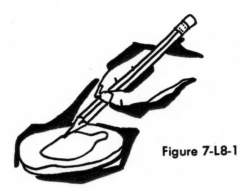

Figure 7-L8-1

4. Incise through the drawn shape, remove excess clay and smooth the clay shape, using one finger moistened in water (Figure 7-L8-2).

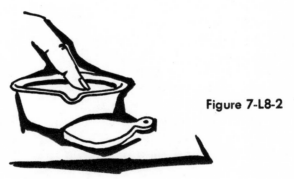

Figure 7-L8-2

5. Select small objects or tools to press textures into the wet clay surface (Figure 7-L8-3).

Figure 7-L8-3

6. Select a powdered-enamel color and spread the powder evenly over the textured clay using a small enamel sifter or pinching it between two fingers (Figure 7-L8-4).

Figure 7-L8-4

7. Use a lollipop stick to drill holes through the wet clay if the jewelry shape is to be suspended from a chain.

8. Allow at least one day for drying before firing the clay shape very slowly in a kiln (Cone 015 to Cone 014). Add chain or colored cord to complete a necklace or use epoxy to add a pin back to the enameled clay piece (Figure 7-L8-5).

Figure 7-L8-5

9. Clean up by throwing away dried clay, restore unused powdered enamels to jars, throw away dirty enameled powders and used newspapers. Clean tools at the sink and scrub desks with a damp towel. Wash up!

Variations:

1. If powdered enamels are not available, the fired ceramic jewelry can be painted with glossy enamel paint and small brushes.

2. Fire the ceramic jewelry and use a glossy, clear varnish to seal the surface, leaving a natural buff-color finish.

Making an Impression

Objectives:

1. To learn to reproduce an image by casting plaster over clay.
2. To learn to create original three-dimensional designs.

Materials:

Ceramic clay, wire, wire cutter, plaster-of-Paris, shoe boxes or similar-sized cardboard boxes; small objects such as wooden sticks; kitchen tools, hardware, large and small plastic mixing bowls, large spoons, water cups, newspapers or oilcloth.

Guidelines:

Want to create an impression on someone? Why not do it aesthetically by casting mixed plaster over an original design you've created to produce a lasting image? With a few pounds of plaster, some moist ceramic clay and numerous old shoe boxes, any number of people can become artistically involved.

The technique of casting plaster over clay is a simple process, beginning with a detailed design pressed into an uneven clay surface. Once moist clay is pressed into the bottom of a strong cardboard box, almost any object can be used to press a design into its soft surface. Once you've created a fairly uneven clay surface by pressing out the clay with the palm of your hand, you are ready to press objects into the surface to create designs.

Use a variety of objects pressed into the clay to overlap and repeat designs. Press deeply so the designs will show when cast.

Mixing plaster is easy because there is no exacting formula to follow. Begin with water in large plastic bowls and gradually sift plaster-of-Paris into the water by hand until the water no longer absorbs the plaster. You will know when this condition occurs, since the plaster will begin to form a mound of dry plaster over the surface of the water. Don't mix the plaster far ahead of the designing phase of the activity. Use a small, plastic margarine bowl to pour the plaster over the clay in each shoe box. You'll probably use from 10 to 25 pounds of plaster for most groups. Wear old clothes and protect desk surfaces with shiny oilcloth or newspapers. Warn the pupils not to touch their eyes with plaster-covered hands.

How to Do It:

1. Distribute boxes, moist clay, objects, and all other materials to pupils at desks covered with thick pads of newspapers or oilcloth. Pour water into large plastic bowls. Each design may use from a pint to a quart of plaster.

2. Press the moist ceramic clay into a shoe box, sculpturing an indented surface on the clay (Figure 7-L9-1).

Figure 7-L9-1

3. Use a variety of objects to press into the wet clay surface (Figure 7-L9-2).

4. Mix plaster-of-Paris into a large plastic bowl (Figure 7-L9-3).

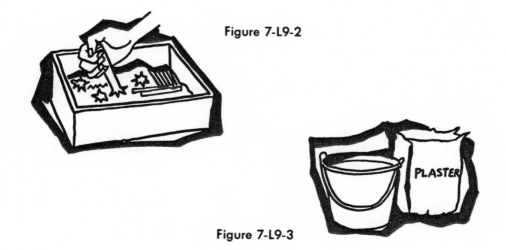

Figure 7-L9-2

Figure 7-L9-3

5. Once the plaster begins to thicken to thin cream consistency, use small plastic bowls to dip the plaster and pour it over the clay designs in boxes. Pre-cut two-inch pieces of small-diameter wire if the casts are to be hung on the wall and embed the wire into the center of the wet plaster (Figure 7-L9-4).

Figure 7-L9-4

6. Dry the plaster slowly, away from heat sources. Allow two to three days to dry thoroughly. Remove the shoe box from the dried plaster and pull the clay away from the cast plaster. Clean the excess clay from the plaster surface.

7. Throw away boxes, newspapers, and scrap materials. Allow the plaster-of-Paris to dry in the plastic bowls before cracking it away from sides and throwing it away outside, then wash the plastic bowls in a sink that has a clean-out trap. Wash up! Avoid touching hands to the eyes or face. Use lots of water to flush out any unusual plaster accidents to the eyes.

Variations:

1. Substitute oil-based clay or sand for the ceramic clay.

2. Glue all the cast impressions together on a piece of masonite or grout, or cement the spaces between individual casts to create a group sculpture.

CHAPTER 8

Found Material Ideas

INTRODUCTION TO "FOUND" MATERIALS

Most young children learn to draw and manipulate simple three-dimensional materials before they enter school. As these pupils progress through elementary school, they learn to construct and design, using more complex three-dimensional materials such as wood, cardboard and clay. All of these three-dimensional activities are extremely vital to the development of spatial awareness and design. Without previous exposure to three-dimensional art, pupils should not be expected to turn out high-level products. Spatial designing is founded upon many learned skills that involve: learning how to fasten a variety of materials together; learning to cut, bend, or shape many different materials; learning to combine different types of materials into a functional, unified design; and learning to construct and design spatially, arranging in space instead of composing visually on a flat surface.

Some young artists instinctively are aware of three-dimensional design and already understand the elements of arranging in space, sometimes without being able to express this knowledge verbally. These pupils can prove invaluable as leaders of various group activities.

Although some subjects or themes lend themselves especially to specific three-dimensional materials, there are few limitations of subject. Three-dimensional art should emphasize imagination and original thinking as much as the areas of painting and drawing. Motivations and demonstrations with found materials are an absolute necessity for

205

most pupils who need some imaginative, open-ended problem to solve. Problems should be presented to groups of pupils in understandable form.

Any new material being introduced to elementary age pupils requires demonstration. It is a good rule to experiment with the material yourself before beginning a new activity. This practice almost always discloses any difficulties that may be encountered by pupils. If you can't do it, don't expect most of the class to be able to!

Found Materials

Found materials are, in reality, scrap materials that must be searched out in attics, basements and garages. Almost any materials light and small enough to carry into school can qualify as art media, but there are some limitations at the elementary school level. Some objects, such as glass, sharp metals, and sharply-pointed objects should be avoided. There is a temptation to provide lists of desirable scrap materials to young pupils, but this frequently proves more limiting than merely discussing open possibilities with the class weeks prior to beginning an activity. Lists seem to force children to look for specific objects, frequently overlooking an unusual piece.

Experiment and exploration are the key concepts when working with found materials. Most dimensional materials are new to pupils and require an incubation period before thinking begins. Don't expect creative thinking to appear spontaneously when new materials are introduced. Allow some time for thought prior to beginning new activities.

Variety is desirable when working with found materials. Even the macaroni used in *Edible Necklaces* can be varied, combined, painted differently, arranged singly, or multiplied. The most simple activity can be varied. Creating aluminum flowers in *Pie Tin Posies* provides the opportunity to use several combinations of materials, creating further variety.

Organizing for Found Materials

All "found material" activities are best organized as group activities in order to share tools, glues and other materials. Some activities require pupils to protect their clothes from spray paint, glue or wheat paste. Plan well ahead of the activity to allow time for pupils to bring in old shirts or smocks.

When rearranging tables or desks pushed together, give some

thought to the placement of pupils. Some children are three-dimensionally oriented and can provide leadership for other pupils in solving the many problems pupils discuss while working in group activities. Disperse your talented pupils effectively among the various groups.

Collecting the materials used in three-dimensional activities requires organizing the class ahead of time. Pupils should understand what they are going to do, and what materials they need prior to beginning the activity. This previous knowledge of the art activity provides ample time for pupils to think about what they want to create. Spontaneity may come easily to the very creative, but most pupils need more time to think before entering into new art activities.

Common Problems in Using Found Materials

There are several problems that pupils encounter when working with found materials. Inexperience with the media is perhaps the most common barrier to creative thought. Pupils need time to explore materials and how they go together. Allow ample time for pupils to think—not always on the day of the activity. Introduce the materials and simple demonstrations prior to beginning lengthy dimensional art activities. These brief introductions will pay dividends in the final stages of the activity.

Pupils may not be familiar with the various types of binding materials used in the various activities. Mixing wheat paste for papier mache to a thick cream consistency, waiting for white glue to dry, and using liquid solder, are all new experiences that require directions and instructions. Plan your instructions step-by-step.

Some dimensional art activities span several art periods or entirely take up one single, lengthy art period. These longer activities should be estimated, time-wise, and planned for thoroughly. Elementary age pupils are not used to phased art activities as their elder peers in junior high school are. Longer art activities require additional teacher motivation and encouragement to sustain the interest of a class.

Working with three-dimensional activities will expose several pupils in the average classroom who are unable to manipulate the materials. These pupils will require additional assistance to complete the activity. This help is better provided by peers than by the teacher. Ask pupil leaders to help those who are encountering difficulties with the activity.

FOUND MATERIAL IDEAS

FOUND MATERIAL ACTIVITY (GRADE LEVEL)	NEW MATERIALS INTRODUCED	PHYSICAL SKILLS INVOLVED	PUPILS LEARN	EMOTIONAL AND INTELLECTUAL EXPERIENCES
Edible Necklaces (Macaroni Jewelry) (K-2)	Enamel spray paint Macaroni	Tieing knots. Stringing small objects on cord. Spraying paint.	To use found materials functionally. To learn about modular materials.	Deciding Elaborating Details
Tin Can Storage (K-2)	Tin cans Enamel paint or contact paper	Spraying paint. Measuring. Cutting sticky paper.	To measure around objects. To use found materials. To create useful objects.	Constructing Elaborating
Pie-Tin Posies (Aluminum Foil Sculpture) (K-3)	Aluminum foil pans Small found objects	Cutting thin metal with scissors. Twisting materials together. Gluing three-dimensional objects.	To create three-dimensional shapes from flat pieces of metal. To elaborate details.	Elaborating Creating Deciding
Pipe Cleaners Go to Work (Mini Papier Mache) (4-6)	Pipe cleaners Wall sizing or wheat paste Masking tape	To build armatures. Stuff bodies. Use masking tape to wrap. Use papier mache. Paint small details.	To create three-dimensionally. To form armatures for small sculpture.	Imagining Creating Originating
Twisted Jewelry (5-6)	Soft wire Wire cutters Jewelry findings Nail polish	Twisting soft wire into designs. Cutting soft wire.	To design jewelry from linear metal material.	Thinking Deciding Creating
Old Glass, New Color (Scrap Bottle Art) (5-6)	Old bottles White glue Colored tissue paper	Overlapping many small torn paper shapes.	About color changes. To use discarded materials functionally.	Selecting Deciding Elaborating
Simple Tree Mobiles (Dipping Cardboard into Plaster) (3-4)	Tree branches Fishing swivels Glitter	Cutting thick paper. Sculpting paper. Adding small details. Balancing weighted objects. Tieing knots.	To create simple balance and movement, using scrap materials.	Changing Adjusting Selecting Deciding
Pressing Out Metal (Embossing Aluminum Foils) (4-6)	Copper or aluminum foil Nails	Pressing out stiff materials. Creating small indentations using nails.	To texture metal surfaces. To create bas-relief sculpture.	Composing Arranging Designing

Edible Necklaces

Objectives:

1. To learn to create original jewelry using found materials.
2. To learn that art can be functional as well as aesthetic.

Materials:

Strong cord or waxed thread, jewelry clasps, several different varieties of macaroni; scissors, paint cans, large plastic bowls, gold enamel spray cans, a length of wire to stretch across a drying area, a large box to spray in, newspapers.

Guidelines:

Looking for a simple, but practical, activity to satisfy that aesthetic urge in you to create? This is the craft activity for you! You'll be surprised at the rich appearance of your macaroni necklace after it has been sprayed with gold metallic paint. Your final craftsmanship will prove practical and worthy enough to present to your favorite person at the proper time!

Not much preparation is necessary to become deeply involved in this crafts activity. There is a certain openness of choice involved in selecting and purchasing pasta shapes used for the basic necklace module. Find a local grocery store that sells a great variety of pasta shapes. Shop carefully! Some pasta shapes may not be sufficiently closed to hold the strand that holds all the pieces together.

You'll need a strong strand of flexible material to string the pasta modules on. Colored macramé cord, thin-plated wire or strong waxed thread will function efficiently. Make certain that your necklace is long enough to fit over your head easily! Fastening the two ends of the necklace can be easily accomplished by purchasing small jewelry clasps to hold the two ends together.

You'll find it fairly easy to push stiff twine or cord through the macaroni pieces. How many pieces of macaroni you'll need to complete your necklace is up to you. A good minimum length for the cord is two or three feet, but you may want to make it longer or create several strands.

There are many ways of decorating your completed strands, but spraying them with gold metallic paint is the most visually appealing. Painting each module a different color by hand with a brush is colorful, but takes longer. Spray paint hangs in the atmosphere, so you need to find a large spraying box to spray into. Hang a paperclip hook on a string from the top of the box to hold each necklace as it is sprayed. Remove the wet necklace and hang it on a wire stretched across an area. Paint may drip, so cover the floor underneath this drying wire rack!

How to Do It:

1. Purchase a variety of macaroni shapes. Pre-cut wire or cord into approximately three-foot, or longer, lengths. Stretch a wire to hang the painted jewelry and cover the floor below this area with newspapers (Figure 8-L1-1).

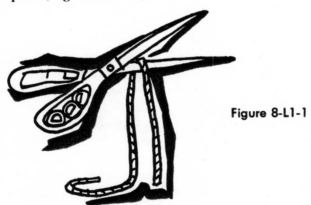

Figure 8-L1-1

2. Prepare a spraying box by pushing an opened paperclip through a large corrugated box to hold each necklace for spraying. Spread newspapers under the box.

3. Distribute the macaroni, cord, and all other materials to small groups of pupils located at tables or desks pushed together to form large working surfaces.

4. Thread the cord through macaroni shapes until you have the proper length desired for a necklace (Figure 8-L1-2).

5. Tie a spring ring to both ends of the necklace or twist wire to fasten the ends together (Figure 8-L1-3).

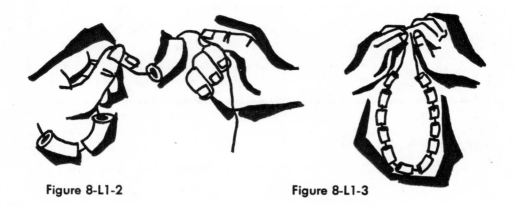

Figure 8-L1-2   Figure 8-L1-3

6. Place the completed jewelry in the spray box and use gold enamel spray paint to coat the pasta (Figure 8-L1-4).

Figure 8-L1-4

7. Remove the sprayed necklace and suspend it from a wire located over newspapers.

8. Clean up by throwing away scraps and newspapers covered with paint. Open the classroom windows to remove the paint odors. Use mild paint thinner to clean off paint on hands and wash with soap and water immediately.

Variations:

1. Insert wooden or glass beads in between the pasta pieces, after they have dried, to create variety and contrast.

2. Suspend an object as a center of interest at the focal point of the necklace.

Tin Can Storage

Objectives:

1. To learn to use found materials creatively and functionally.
2. To learn to measure, plan, and use materials accurately.

Materials:

A roll of self-adhering contact paper, or enamel spray-paint cans; rulers (intermediate grades), 3 small, empty, concentrated-juice cans of various sizes; scissors, elastic bands, newspapers.

Guidelines:

Start drinking concentrated juice in great quantities! Those empty cans can be washed out, covered, and fastened together to produce a functional desk container. Younger pupils in the lower grades may more readily decorate the cans by spraying them with enamel paint rather than by covering them with self-adhering contact paper, since they cannot measure. However, older pupils should become involved in measuring the circumference of the tin cans with strings and rulers and cutting the contact paper themselves. Some pupils, even in intermediate grades, may not be capable of measuring. Plan for individual differences.

Start shopping around for contact paper at your local paint and wallpaper store. Since the juice cans you are going to use are not huge, the pattern on the paper you select should not be very bold or large. Small patterns will provide repetition. Select small patterns!

Start collecting juice cans several weeks before you begin the activity. Store the collected cans until you have a minimum of three cans for each storage project. It might be wise to display to the class a finished tin can storage project containing scissors, pencils and every other object the containers may have to hold! This motivation will provide time to think about the project so that it won't be a surprise.

Be careful when handling the collected juice cans. Not all can openers are perfect! Check carefully to ensure all edges are smooth and that no one will be cut by sharp metal burrs.

Once three juice cans have been completely covered with contact material you can fasten them together in a group using two or three elastic bands. Select the proper size elastic band by testing several different sizes stretched around the circumference. Use white glue to add small dimensional objects to the can, such as plastic flowers, sprigs of pine needles or even old buttons. Be individual!

How to Do It:

1. Collect three concentrated-juice cans for each tin can storage project. Wash cans thoroughly and store them until ready for the activity. Purchase one yard of contact paper.

2. Distribute juice cans, contact paper, elastic bands and scissors to individual pupils at their desks.

3. If primary grades are involved, pre-cut contact paper for the activity or have students spray enamel paint over the metal surface. Pupils who can do so should involve themselves in measuring and creating their own covering material (Figure 8-L2-1).

4. After covering three various-size juice cans with contact paper, stretch several elastic bands around the three cans to hold the cans together (Figure 8-L2-2).

Figure 8-L2-1

Figure 8-L2-2

5. Use white glue to adhere small dimensional objects around the circumference of the decorated cans (optional). (Figure 8-L2-3.)

6. Clean up by saving scrap materials and washing up!

Figure 8-L2-3

Variations:

1. Spray the exteriors of the juice cans with enamel paint and use indelible Magic Markers to create original designs.

2. Use different cans, instead of all the same size, to provide variety.

LESSON 3

Pie Tin Posies

Objectives:

1. To introduce crafts to very young pupils.

2. To learn to use found materials in creating dimensional designs.

Materials:

Small aluminum pot-pie pans, scissors, 12-inch pipe cleaners, paper rickrack, buttons, beads, white glue, newspapers.

Guidelines:

Those old, used aluminum pot-pie tins that provided yesterday's meal may provide the major ingredients for tomorrow's craft activity. There are features of the material in this activity that almost guarantee success. For one thing, aluminum foil is easily cut by even the youngest elementary school pupil. Second, aluminum foil is very flexible; this means the material can be easily bent into sculptural shapes by anyone. Aluminum pie tins are a medium for a simple, but effective, crafts activity.

Begin by collecting aluminum foil pans. Don't feel limited to the small pot-pie pans. Whisk away the foil from under that last frozen blueberry pie you finished. Large foil shapes may stimulate more unusual creative thoughts! Some of your aluminum containers may need scrubbing—they may still be sticky with food, especially if you've collected them from young pupils who may have neglected to inform their mothers why they needed them!

A little motivation may be necessary to encourage thinking about how aluminum foil can be turned into flowers or other forms. Perhaps a sample or two will help younger pupils to begin to incubate three-dimensional ideas. If we cut the foil this way, it creates legs and turns into an imaginary animal. That round pot-pie pan will create a beautiful flower when cut through the center. Stick a strong pipe cleaner through for a stem!

This is a simple craft activity. The only minor problem may be encountered when you attempt to punch a hole through foil. Punching the hole is easy enough, but avoiding the points of the scissors as it passes through the foil may not be as simple!

Start thinking about how to utilize all those beautiful, shiny, metal shapes you have on your hands. Why not create a large three-dimensional bulletin board so that all your artists are involved in a mural? Start thinking about a background to display your metal foil creations.

How to Do It:

1. Collect a variety of aluminum foil pans from frozen pot-pies, fruit pies, and frozen dinners. Wash out any pans that require cleaning.

2. Distribute aluminum foil pans, scissors, two 12-inch pipe cleaners, white glue and other materials to pupils at tables.

3. Use a sharp pair of scissors to demonstrate how to cut through a thin foil surface. To create flowers, cut at an angle directly through to the center of the foil, leaving a center circle (Figure 8-L3-1).

4. Continue cutting through the foil at an angle until the pan is completely cut (Figure 8-L3-2).

5. Use the points of scissors to punch a hole through the center

Figure 8-L3-1   Figure 8-L3-2

of the foil. Twist two pipe cleaners together to form a stem and pass it through the hole. Tie a knot close to the top of the twisted stem and a button (Figure 8-L3-3).

6. Use white glue to fasten beads or buttons to the center of the aluminum foil flower, or twist the pipe cleaner stems through the beads. Allow ample time for the glue to set (Figure 8-L3-4).

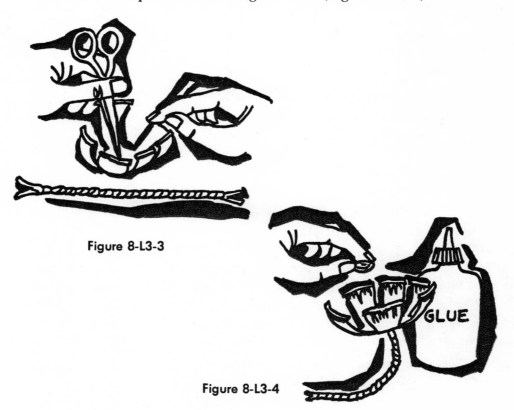

Figure 8-L3-3

Figure 8-L3-4

7. Clean up excess white glue on desks with a damp sponge. Save usable scraps for the scrap box and throw away junk pieces. Wash up with soap and water.

Variations:

1. Combine all the aluminum foil flowers into a mural by stapling the pipe cleaner stems to a prepared bulletin board background.

2. Create a suspended mobile from the aluminum foil sculpture.

LESSON 4

Pipe Cleaners Go to Work

Objectives:

1. To simplify three-dimensional papier mache sculpture.

2. To learn to create imaginary animals.

Materials:

Chenille (thick) pipe cleaners, small widths of masking tape, scissors, wheat paste, water cups, water, cotton batten, small paint brushes, tempera paint, paper towels, plastic bowls, newspapers.

Guidelines:

Take a close look at the reason you select various art activities for your pupils. Have you ever had your pupils spend many hours and days creating large papier mache animals and then wondered if they wouldn't have been as satisfied with smaller ones? Although we may think of sculpture in terms of large objects, sometimes the same educational objectives can be met just as easily in smaller size, in much less time. Why waste hours creating a two-foot monster when you can introduce your pupils to the same skills in less than half the time? Once the idea of miniature sculpture has penetrated through traditional concepts of large size, you may discover that small three-dimensional sculpture has the same educational value as larger sculpture.

In miniature sculpture, doubled pipe cleaners twisted together are substituted for the usual rolled newspaper armatures in animal bodies and legs. What animals? Why do your pupils need to try to imitate realistic animal shapes? Why not imaginary ones? Frustrations can be pushed aside by thinking about "glob" animals. Who knows, after all, what a "glob" animal is supposed to look like? If you don't know what it looks like, you probably won't be wrong when you create it!

If this is your first trip into the world of papier mache, it may be necessary to acquire some basic skills first before attempting any creative thinking about imaginary three-dimensional animals! Practice twisting pipe cleaners into various shapes first.

How to Do It:

Following motivations about imaginary animals:

1. Organize the class into groups of four or five pupils each at tables, or desks pushed together. Cover the table with newspaper.

2. Mix wheat paste in a plastic bowl to a creamy consistency (Figure 8-L4-1).

3. Distribute a minimum of ten 12-inch, chenille pipe cleaners, scissors, small diameter mastic or scotch tape to each pupil and wheat paste in bowls, water cups, newspapers and cotton batten to pupils organized in small groups.

4. Twist several chenille pipe cleaners together to create strong armatures for legs, bodies, necks and heads. You may have to twist several lengths together for the body and head sections of some animals (Figure 8-L4-2).

Figure 8-L4-2

Figure 8-L4-1

5. Once the basic body, legs and heads of the imaginary animal have been twisted together firmly to create a basic shape, it can be padded with cotton batten to round out the body (Figure 8-L4-3).

6. With the cotton batten on the body firmly wrapped with tape, apply small torn strips of newspaper or paper toweling over the padded shape. Dip each individual piece of newspaper strip into prepared wheat paste. Wrap the strip around the body form, overlapping each strip to create a firm body (Figure 8-L4-4).

Figure 8-L4-3

Figure 8-L4-4

7. Use paper toweling, or a different material, to add additional layers over the first. Two, or sometimes three, layers of paper are usually sufficient.

8. Place the completed papier mache animal on newspapers to dry.

9. Once the completed animal shape has dried, use tempera paint to decorate its surface (Figure 8-L4-5).

Figure 8-L4-5

10. Clean up by throwing away scrap materials, washing brushes, and water cups. Rinse wheat paste outdoors to avoid clogging sinks. Store usable materials and wash up!

Variations:

1. Organize pupils into groups to work cooperatively on large papier mache sculpture, using wood nailed together with chicken wire as an armature.

2. Create a large diorama of the small imaginary animals, complete with three-dimensional background.

LESSON 5

Twisted Jewelry

Objectives:

1. To learn to bend and twist soft metal wire to create original jewelry.

2. To learn to create three-dimensional designs.

Materials:

Spools of soft wire, metal chain, used jewelry findings, scissors (or wire cutters), clear nail polish, newspapers.

Guidelines:

Have you ever envied those creative persons who so easily construct, build, design and originate most of their possessions? Why envy them? Why not join them?

There's a beginning for everyone and everything. Here is one of the best ways to create your own original jewelry. Anyone who can twist soft wire is eligible! Twisted jewelry requires only a length of soft wire, some old metal chain from some discarded junk jewelry and a bit of patience.

Soft wire is a vague description so let's take a further look at which types of wire may be best for your jewelry. Copper and lead-tin wires are soft and pliable as are some brass-coated wires. Test the malleability of your wire first by bending it, then straightening the wire back into its original shape. If the wire bends back into shape easily, you have the material you need for twisted jewelry.

The diameter, or thickness, of your wire is very important. Wire for twisted jewelry should be a minimum of 1/8 of an inch, up to 1/4 of an inch in diameter. Any thinner gauge is difficult to work with.

You'll need a wire cutter for some wires, but if you are using a soft solder wire, ordinary scissors will cut through the metal with little harm to the scissors blades. Some wires may need a little shining and polishing, but you may also like the antique effect of aged wire. If you do decide to polish your wire, protect the polished wire surface with a coating of clear nail polish for lasting brilliance.

Search around in old jewelry boxes for "findings" (a jewelry term for metal pieces such as rings and hooks). You'll need a "spring" ring to fasten both ends of your necklace chain to and an "S" ring, or circle, to hold your twisted wire pendant. Substitutes for these findings may be created from the soft metal itself.

If you have never worked with wire before, perhaps a few minutes of practice or a lot of demonstrated samples are in order. Perhaps both!

How to Do It:

1. Organize pupils into small groups to share tools and materials. Cover tables with pads of newspaper. Distribute materials to groups.

2. Cut soft wire into 12, 16, and 20-inch lengths using a wire cutter. If the wire is dull, draw it through steel wood and wipe excess bits of metal off with a soft cloth (Figure 8-L5-1).

3. Demonstrate how soft wire can be easily rolled into circular shapes, or twisted into open shapes (Figure 8-L5-2).

Figure 8-L5-1   **Figure 8-L5-2**

4. Twist your piece of soft wire into an original design. Use scissors to cut away any excess wire.

5. Fasten jewelry chains and rings to complete your necklace (Figure 8-L5-3).

Figure 8-L5-3

6. Place newspapers under the completed necklace and use clear nail polish to coat the metal surface (optional).

7. Hang the coated jewelry to dry, suspended from a stretched wire in an isolated corner.

8. Throw away small scraps. Collect materials and use nail polish remover if pupils have spilled nail polish. Wash up using soap and hot water!

Variations:

1. Once pupils have experienced creating wire jewelry, they may be introduced to more advanced wire-bending and twisting activities such as wire sculpture or mobiles.

LESSON 6

Old Glass, New Cover

Objectives:

1. To learn to create functional art from found materials.

2. To learn to design, using a variety of materials.

Materials:

Oddly-shaped bottles, colored tissue paper, old easel brushes, thinned white glue or decoupage liquid, a stick for stirring glue, clear plastic spray, paper towels, newspapers, a large box to spray in.

Guidelines:

Begin collecting old jars and glasses from cellars and attics to create your own stained glass vases. A few scraps of colored tissue paper, some white glue, a few old easel brushes combined with discarded bottles become the basis for a simple, but effective, crafts activity.

Although it is possible to cover almost any type of discarded glassware with colored tissue paper, you should give some thought to the final look. How will that classically-shaped bottle, that formerly contained pancake syrup, look covered in oranges and reds? That oddly-shaped, cooking oil or old brandy bottle may prove just right as a vase in blues and greens. Turning your "throw aways" into functional decor makes good sense and good ecology!

You'll need to thin white glue with water until it flows readily. You can accomplish this by gradually adding water to a quart of white glue until the white drips fairly freely from your stirring stick. White glue "picks up" some of the dyes from some types of colored tissue paper. Working quickly in applying tissue paper to the bottles will help to minimize this. Use an easel brush to smooth down the edges of tissue paper on the bottle or these edges will harden into a rough surface.

Overlapping the colored tissue paper and selecting colors are the two keys to success. Success is yours if you pay attention to these simple rules. Tear, rather than cut, irregular paper shapes of colored tissue paper. Tearing creates a different shape from cutting. When torn shapes overlap on a glass surface, they create a myriad of color changes.

Using thinned white glue requires some directions. Wear smocks to protect your clothing. Colored dyes from the tissue paper will discolor your fingers. You may want to keep paper towels nearby to wipe your hands occasionally. Don't worry about the white glue that dries into a hard shell on your fingers. When this glue is completely dried, it can be peeled off—washing with soap and hot water will get rid of the rest!

How to Do It:

1. Prepare white glue by thinning it with water (see previous directions) or use commercial decoupage glue.

2. Distribute the glue in water cups to small groups of pupils at tables. Allow several pupils at a time to select colored tissue paper scraps from a centrally located table. Distribute the remainder of the materials and cover the tables with several layers of newspapers prior to beginning the activity.

3. Tear colored tissue paper into irregular shapes of various sizes and colors (Figure 8-L6-1).

4. Apply the thinned glue to parts of the bottle first. Press the torn tissue shapes into the wet glue and use an easel brush to add a finish coat (Figure 8-L6-2).

Figure 8-L6-1   **Figure 8-L6-2**

5. Apply the damp tissue paper over other parts of the bottle. Use a single finger to smooth the edges of the tissue flat (Figure 8-L6-3).

Figure 8-L6-3

6. Repeat the process with a different-colored tissue paper shape. Overlap the added pieces of tissue paper over the first shapes. Smooth the two pieces of tissue paper. Continue this process until the entire bottle is covered (Figure 8-L6-4).

Figure 8-L6-4

7. Use paper towels to wipe any excess glue from your fingers. Carry the finished glass vase to a drying area covered with newspapers. Wash brushes out in warm soapy water immediately before they become hardened.

8. Clean up by throwing away contaminated glue, discarded materials and small scraps. Save large pieces for the scrap box. Peel dried white glue from fingers and wash up using soap and water.

Variations:

1. Paint small designs over the colored tissue paper base and display the completed vase in front of the window to take advantage of the semi-transparency.

2. Cover flat plastic shapes similarly to create a form of stained glass design.

LESSON 7

Simple Tree Mobiles

Objectives:

1. To introduce the concept of balance and movement.

2. To learn to create beginning mobiles from simple materials.

Materials:

Small pieces of heavy paper, scissors, a colored crayon, small birch branches, white thread, plastic pails, fishing swivels, several screw eyes, water, glitter, tempera paint, small brushes, water cups, heavy stranded wire to stretch across the room, newspapers.

Guidelines:

Want to hang your art up high where everyone can see it? This is the activity to think about if you've never been exposed to the complexities of balance and movement. Since these two concepts are the important objectives of the activity, expend less time and effort creating the suspended objects of the mobiles.

There are lots of materials to be collected for mobile making. Begin by gathering small tree branches. Find the balance of the branch by holding it suspended on one finger. A simple screw eye and a fishing swivel from a friend will add the necessary hardware to suspend this basic piece of your mobile from a wire stretched across the room. The stretched wire should be heavy and strong enough to suspend several mobiles.

Fishing swivels play an important role in mobile making because they allow each suspended piece to turn independently. Many school mobiles turn out to be "stabiles" since they can revolve only a few inches in one direction, then reverse, soon stopping entirely. Fishing swivels permit a complete 360-degree turn of each suspended object.

You can suspend almost any lightweight object from a small mobile, but if it's your first experience at mobiles, keep it simple! Cut a free shape from lightweight board or heavy paper, string it, curl it, paint it, throw some glitter on the wet surface, and you have a quick object to suspend from your mobile. Once your abstract mobile shape dries, you are ready to tie the whole thing together. Suspend one object at a time and don't tie any permanent knots to the branch until all the suspended objects are in place.

The objects that you suspend from your mobile can be hung with small fishing swivels and paper clips. The length of the fine white thread used to hang the object depends upon where the suspended object is finally placed on the mobile. These pieces must be adjusted to turn freely without touching one another.

You'll need a partner, or two, to share the tasks involved in creating a mobile. Several hands are required! Don't try to complete group mobiles in one day. Rome took longer, you know! There are several phases the activity can be divided into: (1) hanging the tree branch requires two people for each mobile; (2) everyone can create his own individual object to be suspended, and, finally; (3) small groups become involved in balancing the final mobile. These three phases can be accomplished at three separate times or stretched over one long time period.

Think about mobiles first, create later!

How to Do It:

1. Organizing the materials days before the activity begins allows time to phase the activity over several class periods or days.

2. During the first phase of mobile making, stranded wire should be stretched across the classroom above the height of the pupils, but low enough to reach up to.

3. Use your forefinger to find the balance of each individual small branch.

4. Fasten small screw eyes (approximately 3/8-inch in diameter) at the balance of the branch. Twist picture frame wire into a screw eye and attach a fishing swivel (Figure 8-L7-1).

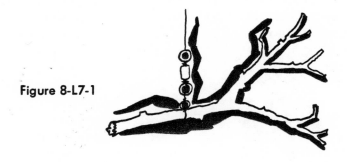

Figure 8-L7-1

5. Hang the tree branch from the wire stretched across the room. (Option: the branch may be sprayed with paint prior to this phase of the activity.)

6. Following the balancing phase, organize and distribute the materials to be used to create the suspended shapes. Distribute scissors, paper, paint, glitter and other materials to groups of pupils at tables covered with newspapers.

7. Cut heavy paper into free-form shapes; cut through parts of the shape and curl it to create three-dimensional forms. Use a sharp object to drill a hole through the paper (Figure 8-L7-2).

Figure 8-L7-2

Figure 8-L7-3

8. Cut and tie a piece of thread through the hole. Paint designs on the open shape using brightly colored tempera paint and small watercolor brushes. Add glitter or texture to the wet surface at this phase (Figure 8-L7-3).

9. Following this phase, reorganize the class to demonstrate the principles of balanced weight. Show how balance is accomplished by suspending various shapes (all hung from fishing swivels) on the tree branch (Figure 8-L7-4). Allow ample space between each suspended object to permit complete 360-degree turns. Moving mobiles are more interesting; swivels are the only device that will allow complete 360-degree circular movement.

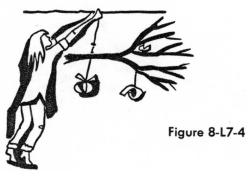

Figure 8-L7-4

10. Clean up by throwing away small scraps. Wash paint brushes in warm water and shape each point before drying. Wash up and open up the windows to watch the air move your balanced mobile!

Variations:

1. Suspend other simple, light objects such as pencils, objects from nature, or thin wire sculpture.

2. Have each pupil create his own smaller individual mobile.

LESSON 8

Pressing Out Metal

Objectives:

    1. To learn to create simple bas-relief.

    2. To learn to design using different materials.

Materials:

Rolls of thin copper or aluminum foil, boxwood tools, pads of newspapers, scotch tape, manila paper, pencils, crayons, nails.

Guidelines:

Embossing, that is, pressing a design out in relief, is a valuable form of three-dimensional art to learn from since it introduces the concept of depth in one easy activity. Before you progress up to the sculptural level of Michelangelo, you need more experiences with semi-dimensional techniques such as embossing. Embossing is a simple activity using tools with which you press out partly three-dimensional designs from the reverse side of thin sheets of metal foil. All you need to begin are the right tools, materials and attitude!

Most sheets of metal foil can be embossed, using hard, boxwood tools. Soft wooden materials, such as lollipop sticks, will break under the pressure. Only hardwood tools, such as boxwood ceramic tools, will withstand this pressure.

Selecting the right thickness of metal foil is crucial. There are no hard and fast rules that are available to help you select the right foil. Some pupils can press out heavier-gauge copper materials. but most elementary school pupils need to work with commercial aluminum materials specifically designed for embossing. These can be found listed in any handicraft supply catalog. Ordinary kitchen foil is much too thin for embossing and is easily torn by the wooden tools.

Begin by sketching your ideas on manila paper. Drawing directly on the metal foil is not advisable since errors cannot be erased.

Think out your visual idea or design before embossing it on the metal permanently.

You'll need a very thick pad of newspapers underneath your metal foil. The height of your final relief will be limited to half the thickness of your pad of newspapers. So, if you want to really create a high relief design, you should stack quite a pad of newspapers underneath your metal foil.

One major thought. Take it easy! Embossing requires you to press on the reverse side of your metal surface. Your action pushes, or extrudes, the front surface of the metal outwardly. It is far better to push out the surface slowly than to ruin your design by exerting too much pressure. Use your hard wooden tool to outline the design after you have traced it onto the metal. Working from the outer edge of the drawn design, inwardly, is the best way.

You may encounter some difficulty pressing out the metal. Check carefully to ascertain that: (1) the newspaper pad underneath the foil is at least two inches thick; (2) the foil you are using is sufficiently soft and malleable; (3) the wooden tool that you are using is hard enough to push out the metal.

You can "antique" the final embossing by rubbing some acrylic paint over the metal surface and wiping the excess off. This produces an "aged" effect that contrasts to the bright metal surface.

How to Do It:

1. Pre-cut metal foil into a variety of sizes ranging from 4 × 6-inches to 6 × 8-inches. Cut manila paper the same size.

2. Use a crayon to sketch a design on the pre-cut manila paper. Pencils produce designs that are too small to emboss (Figure 8-L8-1).

3. Once the crayon design is completed, use scotch tape to tape the design over a piece of metal foil. Use a hard pencil or small pointed metal tool to outline the design (Figure 8-L8-2).

Figure 8-L8-1

Figure 8-L8-2

4. Remove the paper original. Turn over the metal on the paper pad and use a hardwood tool to "push out" the back of the design. Begin by working around the perimeter of the design to the center (Figure 8-L8-3).

5. Use common nails or other sharp pointed tools to create a contrasting surface texture. Press the metal points sharply into the metal surface (Figure 8-L8-4).

Figure 8-L8-3

Figure 8-L8-4

6. Rub brown or black paint over the metal surface, let it set a moment, and wipe *some of the paint* off the highlights of the design. Test this step before demonstrating to pupils (Figure 8-L8-5).

Figure 8-L8-5

7. Carry the completed design to a drying area. Wash up and throw away excess materials. Save metal scraps for collage materials.

Variations:

1. Completed embossed designs can be mounted on wood by using small metal brads.

INDEX